THE SAN FRANCISCO MIME TROUPE PRESENTS...

By Popular Demand

PLAYS AND OTHER WORKS BY

THE SAN FRANCISCO MIME TROUPE

SAN FRANCISCO
1980

Copyright © 1970, 1971, 1975, 1978, 1980
by the San Francisco Mime Troupe, Inc.
All rights reserved, including professional, amateur, motion picture,
public reading and translation. For all production and other rights,
please address the San Francisco Mime Troupe, 855 Treat Street,
San Francisco, California 94110.
Library of Congress Catalog Card Number 79-93008.

2

Prologue

THIS BOOK holds the bricks needed to build a very special sort of theater — well, some of the bricks. The reader must furnish voices, gestures, a setting, the feel of the audience. It may help, then, to introduce the San Francisco Mime Troupe as well as introducing this book.

The name confuses people. They think 'mime' means 'silent,' and expect a group of white-faced jumpsuits climbing imaginary stairs behind invisible walls, rather than the extremely articulate, music-making, even noisy actors whose words are recorded here. The company has a standard official explanation, distinguishing mime from pantomime (which is silent), and Chaplin from Marceau, but the real reason for obstinately keeping a name which may mislead is a pardonable pride in being San Francisco's oldest theater company (twenty years in 1979), with a countryful of friends and supporters.

The Mime Troupe goes where people are — walks into a park, puts up signs, sets up its stage, makes music, presents a play. Lights do not dim, there is no rustle of programs, no last minute coughing or polite hush. No curtain.

Everything about this theater is direct. It has no invisible 'fourth wall.' Actors look right at, speak directly to, the audience as well as each other. The actors are present, not hidden behind the characters, who — presidents and peons, agitators and ambassadors, B-girls and bosses — are drawn boldly, to the edge of caricature. Broad gestures, a farcical approach reinforce this boldness; costumes, masks, makeup are used not to elaborate but to typify the character; music works to underline, not distract. And — as the scripts here show — the political intention is explicit, never disguised.

This honesty creates a sort of complicity with those who have stayed to watch. People can, and usually do, comment on the action — not just booing and cheering, though that too, but advising on real choices within the play.

There is another important level of communication: after the play is over, the actors ask for money. Clearly, if the company is to survive, it must be flexible and quick to provide the audience with something it wants.

This means listening closely to the audience before it is an audience, discovering what people feel is important now. And that means the plays in this book, which covers seven years of work, concern the price of beans, rapid transit, heroin, culture from above, laughter from below, equal rights for women, sex, death, race, imperialism and more.

Another part of the task is finding a form the audience can respond to. In trying to reach all the people (with subjects which affect all the people) the company has consciously, deliberately, used a number of dramatic styles, and the plays here include melodrama, vaudeville, circus turns, mystery adventure — even realism.

Despite all the shifts from topic to topic and form to form, the plays have a strong central similarity: they are political plays, as they concern the ways people deal with each other and with their government; they are plays of protest, as they concern the ways people and governments abuse people. They usually end hopefully, but only hopefully — we are still in this world, people are still misused, abused. And they make us laugh, in the belief that laughter gives us the distance to understand, and understanding brings the desire to work for change.

Here then are four plays and four actos, chosen from some twenty Mime Troupe productions between 1970 and 1976 — chosen partly for their ability to survive the transition to the printed page, partly because they give some idea of the variety of responses brought to a variety of problems.

In performance, the company is fluid. Lines change, so these printed scripts can provide only a good example of particular plays.

Some of the pieces may seem to suffer now from the immediacy which once made them so valuable — Nixon and Ford are (today) resting in the sun, but out of the limelight; the war in Southeast Asia is apparently over — but that requires no apology: the plays work both as history and as models for dealing with the next face of the enemy. Other pieces are offered partly as examples of a specific device (a paper movie in *Los Siete*, juggling in *Frozen Wages*) or style — *San Fran Scandals* may appear parochial, but its splendid vaudeville approach would fit any time, any where, many older people are displaced for the pleasure or profit of a few.

Shorter, simpler pieces alternate with more elaborate productions from season to season. *Eco-Man* demonstrates the possibility of using a simple form without sacrificing power; it can be performed by three people in almost any open space. *The Dragon Lady's Revenge* demonstrates the virtues of complexity: using the familiar and complicated trappings of the hard-to-believe spy film (in this case at high speed, with music) to dissect a story of hard-to-believe foreign intrigue.

The Independent Female lives — the play has been performed successfully by dozens of groups over the years. The 'oldest' play in the book, it remains pungent, funny and timely, but its humor, its style, assume a familiarity with white mainstream culture. In contrast, the most recent pieces here, *Frijoles* and *False Promises/Nos Engañaron*, reflect a multi-racial company's attempts to reach a multi-racial audience. They also demonstrate the possibility of delivering a strong message with airy fantasy (*Frijoles* covered three continents on a few square yards of grass in front of a painted screen) and with earnest realism (several scenes in *False Promises/Nos Engañaron* are nearly naturalistic).

This last play — first in the book, as scripts are presented in reverse chronological order within each section — is the longest, most peopled play here. Its characters seem to have more flesh. Yet this play grows logically from the understanding that informs all the plays: these characters are written and played to make a point, however sympathetic they may be. Even the most realistic scenes keep us, and the characters, aware of the objective history in the play.

* * *

If scripts only suggest a play, then the songs included in this book barely hint at the importance of music. The Mime Troupe is a musical theater. Music has been used in a great variety of ways: most simply to attract passersby, at first marching as a 'Gorilla Band,' more recently by sitting and playing very well. Within the plays, music is used to make character statements, to extend and bolster visual effects past the boundaries of the stage, as comic punctuation, to reiterate the style of a scene or of the whole play.

In the most recent productions, music is less generic, with songs giving actor-characters a chance to reflect aloud, or to enunciate ideas which risk being too simple in straight speech. There is not room here for complete scores, but the book includes lead sheets for eight of the most important songs.

Some sense of the 'stage picture' which the company presents is offered in a short series of photographs from its adaptation of *The Mother* by Bertolt Brecht.

6

[PROLOGUE]

Moving into (and out of) the parks with any sort of speed in a small truck has created very special problems in set design. Some of the solutions, ranging from the elementary to the super-ingenious, are presented in a separate section which speaks quite coherently for itself.

* * *

And now, together again for the first time anywhere, the San Francisco Mime Troupe proudly presents eight plays, some music, handsome pictures, helpful drawings — the fruits of seven years' work to make a free, practical, responsive theater.

— PETER SOLOMON

Acknowledgements

First, to our audience, whose enthusiasm — and well-placed criticism — have given the Mime Troupe its long life.

To those close friends of the company who unfailingly turn up to help it over rough spots. They build sets, hang lights, raise cash, mail flyers, fix cars, roofs, wiring, pipes. They give us confidence when we need it most, and we take this occasion to thank them.

This book would never have seen the light of day without direct help from many people. Howard Dratch pulled it out of a hole. Randall Craig, Barry Glick, Phil Marsh and Javier Pacheco were kind enough to allow us to print songs they wrote for our shows; Patrick Lofthouse, Susan Lyne and Jane Norling contributed posters they designed.

When the book was only an idea, far-sighted people at the Vanguard Foundation (twice!) provided funds to get it moving. W. H. and Carol Ferry also helped generously at this early stage, as did Keith Roberts and Sally Lilienthal. When inflation made our budget obsolete, grants from the Harlyn Foundation, the Community Arts Distribution Committee of the Zellerbach Family Fund, the Mortimer Fleishhacker Foundation and the Wallace Alexander Gerbode Foundation made it possible to finish the job.

Finally, two of the company's oldest friends worked as designer and editor of this book. Capturing the Troupe's color and variety on a black and white page has been the task of Charles A. Bigelow — designer, typographer and fan. His ingenuity and craft are visible on every page; for the consideration and tolerance that don't show, we thank him also. Peter Solomon did not simply edit this book, he made it happen, and we thank him for more work, more forbearance and more generosity than anyone — even a collective — ever had a right to expect.

See you in the parks.

CONTENTS

FOUR PLAYS

THE SAN FRANCISCO MIME TROUPE IN
FALSE PROMISES/NOS ENGAÑARON

CHARACTERS

A BARBER. *Registrar of Voters in a Small Southern Town*
A CUSTOMER
WASHINGTON JEFFERSON. *A Blacksmith; Later, a Soldier*
A VOTER
WILLIAM MCKINLEY. *President of the United States*
J. P. MORGAN. *King of Finance Capital*
THEODORE ROOSEVELT. *Assistant Secretary of the Navy; Later
  Colonel; Still Later, Vice-President*
TOMÁS OROPEZA. *A Miner*　　TOMÁS' FRIEND
HARRY POTTER. *A Miner*
ED CASEY. *A Miner, and a Socialist*
RUBY. *A Dancehall Girl*
CHARLIE SLADE. *President of the Copper City Miners' Union*
BELLE HAYWARD. *A Singer*　　MONTANA. *A Saloonkeeper*
A MINER　　　　　　　　　　TWO MOURNERS
MARIA ROBLEDO. *A Miner's Widow*
A NEWSVENDOR　　　　　　THREE ROUGH RIDERS
FIRST DEPUTY
A BARKEEPER IN PUERTO RICO
A MUSICIAN　　　　　　　　MARITZA. *A Striker*
SECOND STRIKER　　　　　 A LIEUTENANT
SARAH. *A Backsliding Housewife*
DAVEY HAYWARD. *Belle's Brother*
A BACKSLIDING MINER　　　SECOND DEPUTY

Note: The Mime Troupe's contribution to the Bicentennial celebration. Opened July 4, 1976, at a fair and rally in San Francisco's Dolores Park involving some 50 Bay Area radical and community groups.

Historical note: The Spanish-Cuban-American War, which lasted six weeks, resulted in the annexation by the United States of Puerto Rico, the Philippines and Guam and the economic takeover of Cuba. It was followed by the war to conquer the Philippines, which lasted four years.

The strike in the play is based on events in Coeur d'Alene, Idaho, Cripple Creek, Colorado, and Morenci, Arizona, during this period. The characters of Charlie Slade and Ed Casey are drawn from actual figures in the Western Federation of Miners.

False Promises
Nos Engañaron

PROLOGUE

A barber shop and polling place,
Backwater, South Carolina; Election Day, 1896.
American flag preset. Barber enters
with shaving equipment and sign, 'Vote Here.'
Customer enters, takes seat for shave.

CUSTOMER.
Well, Clemson — how you think it's going to come out? Is big business going to take over the country?
BARBER. No, sir — the people's man is going to win.
CUSTOMER. I read where J. P. Morgan led ten thousand bankers in their top hats down Fifth Avenue in New York, for McKinley.
BARBER. Well, sir, them ten thousand bankers in New York probably cost ol' McKinley a hundred thousand votes in the rest of the country. I tell you business is scared.
CUSTOMER. All the niggers going to vote for McKinley. I hear he put out against lynching.
BARBER. Did he now? Well, there ain't going to be no niggers voting in this election, in this town or anywhere else in the South. This is the year the white man starts to take back his own.
Washington Jefferson enters.
What you want?
JEFFERSON. I come to vote.
CUSTOMER. Here's a nigger wants to get himself killed.

13

BARBER. I got news for you, boy. We got us a brand-new state constitution. If you want to vote in this election, I got to give you a few tests.

White voter enters.

VOTER. Mr. Simpson done sent me down here to vote again and I'm supposed to hurry up and get back to work.

JEFFERSON. The line forms behind me.

CUSTOMER. This nigger don't know when to stop.

BARBER. Now hold on. First off, can't no man vote in this election 'less his grandaddy was a registered voter prior to 18 and 65.

JEFFERSON. Was Colonel Theotus Jefferson, of the Belle Reeve plantation, a registered voter?

BARBER. The Colonel, rest his soul, was a lifelong Democrat. What's he got to do with you voting?

JEFFERSON. What he did with my grandmama has to do with me voting.

VOTER. He got you there, Clem — fair and square.

JEFFERSON. You gonna ask him about his grandaddy?

VOTER. I don't know who he was — shoot, my grandma don't, neither.

BARBER. You a real smart boy, ain't you, boy? Let's see how smart you can do the new literacy test. Can you read the United States Constitution? *Hands him book.*

JEFFERSON. *Reads.* Article 15, Section 1. The right of any citizen to vote shall not be denied or abridged by reason of race, color, or previous condition of servitude.

CUSTOMER. *Rises and takes book.* Well! You passed the tests. Passed 'em fair and square, so we're going to be fair with you. Down here in South Carolina, we got ourselves two kinds of ballots...

Barber displays them.

... we got lots of nice, clean, Democratic ballots with William Jennings Bryan on 'em, and we got a few raggedy old Republican ballots with William McKinley. And we

14

are all mighty curious, ain't we, boys?

They are.

— to see which one a smart, uppity nigger is going to choose. Come on now, nigger — you going to be uppity, or you going to be smart?

JEFFERSON. Give me a Republican ballot.

VOTER. Jefferson, you're a dumb nigger.

BARBER. *Hits Jefferson over the head with the flag.* Get a clean sheet! Go call the boys!

Barber and voter drag Jefferson off.

CUSTOMER. Looks like there's going to be a lynching. *Exits.*

Offstage: men shout, women scream, dogs bark.

VOICE. Watch out! The nigger's got a gun!

Gunshot, screams.

Jefferson enters, running, with smoking gun.

JEFFERSON. That was a close shave. I got to get out of here. Y'all stay, plant your feet, take a seat, and dig your roots, as the San Francisco Mime Troupe presents: FALSE PROMISES/NOS ENGAÑARON: in other words, we been had. *Exits.*

I. 1

Washington, DC, early in 1898.
Backstage: Cries for war.
McKinley enters.

MCKINLEY.

Cease this heedless clamor
To drive us into an immoral war
Before we're ready!
You think it's easy, being President?
Cuba, a fragrant island off our coast,
Has risen in revolt against the Spanish
And asks our aid. Now, Wall Street wants no war —
Wants no disruption of serene investment —
But empire-builders want all Spain has left!
Lord, show me the true path midst this confusion.
                    Theodore Roosevelt enters.
ROOSEVELT. Mr. President!
MCKINLEY.   Not now, Roosevelt.
ROOSEVELT. I've brought you a jim-dandy battle plan!
MCKINLEY. What for?
ROOSEVELT.   For war with Spain.
MCKINLEY. You see how they torment me?
                    Knock, knock, knock.
                    Oh — *Irritated* — who knocks?
                    J. P. Morgan enters.
MORGAN. Who rules on Wall Street?
MCKINLEY. 'Tis J. P. Morgan.
ROOSEVELT.   King of high finance.
                    Roosevelt and McKinley bow.
MORGAN. McKinley, I'll be brief — I always am.
I speak for capital. We want new markets.
ROOSEVELT. Sir, Wall Street's seen the light on Cuba.
MORGAN. Cuba's a speck, not worth consideration.
We want China.

Roosevelt inhales.

MCKINLEY. But I have sworn that while I'm President,
America will launch no overseas
Adventures.

ROOSEVELT.   China!

MCKINLEY. *To Roosevelt.* Do you think we could?

MORGAN. We don't need countries, we need customers.
Dream — millions of Chinese, all wearing Levi's.

MCKINLEY. Lord, show Thy servant how to gain new
markets.

ROOSEVELT. I'll show you how to get the China trade.
Morgan and McKinley are all ears.
You start in Cuba.
They are disgusted.
Shows map.   Soon as war breaks out,
Our Army mounts a double-pronged attack:
Cuba and Porto Rico. Our Atlantic fleet
Attacks their Navy in the Caribbean.
Meanwhile, from Hong Kong, our Pacific squadron
Sets out full steam ahead —

MORGAN.   Hong Kong?

MCKINLEY.   What squadron?
What STEAM? Our Navy's still in sailing ships!

ROOSEVELT. Not so, sir. As Assistant Secretary,
I've built a first-class modern Navy. Now —
Pacific squadron
Full steam ahead, straight to the Philippines.

MORGAN. The Philippines?

MCKINLEY.   What's that?

MORGAN. A group of islands — off the China coast!

MORGAN & MCKINLEY. Let me see that map!

ROOSEVELT. Spain's richest colony — also in revolt.

MORGAN. McKinley, our possession of these islands
Would guarantee an Open Door to China.

ROOSEVELT. He sees — our destiny is manifest:

To liberate Spain's island colonies
And then to keep them.
MCKINLEY. We are a Christian nation! We don't conquer
At will and whim! We need a good excuse.
ROOSEVELT. The Maine could cruise to Cuba's coast, and find
one.
MCKINLEY. *Suddenly transfixed.* Gentlemen, I hear a call. His
voice!
He's telling me our country has been chosen
To aid brave Cuba's noble fight for freedom.
Thy holy mission we accept, oh Lord:
We'll teach democracy with fire and sword. *Exits.*
ROOSEVELT. Now that's the ticket! We're a fighting race,
As all great races have been. We must conquer,
Or else decay, and lose our manly vigor.
Forward — now sound the trumpet, bleat the tuba!
I shall not rest till victory in Cuba. *Exits.*

18

MORGAN. Each lackey thinks HE's making history. Ha!
Now cries for war will ring from press and pulpit,
Fleets will sink, lands burn, governments collapse,
While big banks take all in. I'm off to Wall Street.
Once, there was risk in business — now, not much.
The more we steal, the less we can be touched.

I. 2

A mine head, Copper City, Colorado, February 1898.
Tomás and friend enter, wipe their faces, squint at the light.
Harry and Casey follow. Harry sees Tomás.

HARRY.

Hey, you! Pancho!

TOMÁS. It's Señor Oropeza, pendejo.

HARRY. Yeah? You know you nearly killed me down there
today? Hey, Casey! Half the roof caved in after this dumb
son-of-a-bitch got done moving the timbers.

Copper City,
Colorado
Spring 1898

TOMÁS. Is it my fault the company don't provide enough timbers?
His friend tries to calm him.
It's bad enough we get all the shit jobs — I'm tired of taking crap all day long from a bunch of half-drunk hillbillies that don't know a copper mine from a hole in the ground.
HARRY. Hillbilly? Why, you greaseball son of a bitch!
Harry goes for Tomás — Casey holds him back.
Tomás, cursing in Spanish, is dragged off by his friend.
Go to hell, you son of a bitch!
CASEY. You want a fight, go call out one of the managers.
HARRY. We never had half as many accidents till the company hired them damn Mexicans.
CASEY. Where'd you get that piece of news? You were hired after they were.
HARRY. Charlie Slade told me.
CASEY. There's one reason not to believe it.
HARRY. Look, Casey — I don't want to hear no more of your talk against Charlie. Charlie Slade has done a lot for us miners!
CASEY. And us miners have done a lot for Charlie Slade. Charlie don't want the Mexicans in the union, because they don't know those fine stories about Charlie, the hero. They'd have to go by what they'd see.
HARRY. Charlie's down there right now, negotiating with the company, fighting to get us an eight-hour day!
CASEY. Charlie's down there trying to fix it so we don't go on strike, because he knows damn well, even if you don't, that we are never going to win a strike without the Mexicans.
HARRY. *Leaving.* Bullshit!
CASEY. All right — let's go find your friend Charlie.
Exeunt.

I.3

Montana's Last Chance Saloon, Copper City,
that evening. Ruby enters, polishes bar.
Slade enters with newspaper and air of jubilation.

RUBY.
If it ain't the best-dressed union president between Granite
and Leadville! Don't keep us in suspense, Charlie — is there
gonna be a strike?

SLADE. I don't think so.

RUBY. *Suggestively.* In that case, you got time for a nice juicy
steak?

SLADE. Looks like you haven't seen the news. *Hands her paper.*

RUBY. *Reads.* 'Battleship Maine Blown Up in Havana Harbor.' Jesus, Mary and Joseph. '260 Sailors Lost.' Oh, my God. 'Officers Saved.' Well, that's good. 'The Question on Every Lip: Did a Spanish Torpedo Do the Awful Work?'

SLADE. Makes you sick, doesn't it?

RUBY. *Gasps.* Look at this picture! 'Spanish Torpedo,' with an arrow. I guess that proves it, all right.

Belle enters, dusty, with suitcase.

BELLE. Excuse me — I'm looking for Montana.

RUBY. *Examines her dubiously.* Just a moment — I will call her. *Yells.* Montana! Say, Charlie — what was it doing in Havana?

CHARLIE. *Who has been studying Belle.* What was what?

RUBY. The battleship!

Slade shrugs.

To Belle. Want to see the paper?

BELLE. No thanks. I come about a job.

RUBY. *Louder this time.* Montana! *To Belle.* You know, Montana — she don't hire nobody just to be a waitress.

BELLE. That's good, 'cause I don't want to be just a waitress.

RUBY. MONTANA!

Montana enters.

MONTANA. *Louder than Ruby.* DON'T HOLLER LIKE THAT! You can ruin your voice. *Ignoring Belle's stare.* Well, well — labor's hero is home from the wars. Seen the good news, Charlie?

SLADE. I seen it.

MONTANA. Now give me the bad news. You calling 'em out?

RUBY. Montana, this here girl is waiting to see you.

MONTANA. SEE me? She ain't blinked an eye since I walked through the door. What's the matter, honey — eyes ain't used to the dark?

Belle shakes her head.

What you want?

BELLE. I'm a singer.

MONTANA. In church, or on hayrides? Can you dance?

BELLE. Sure! Course, I never had no formal lessons.

MONTANA. Let's see how fast you can learn. Follow Ruby.

Musicians play, Ruby does a fast tap step.
Belle is lost.

Take it a little slower.

Ruby yawns, then takes it a little faster.

Sorry, honey. This is a professional club.

BELLE. But you didn't hear me sing yet!

MONTANA. I don't need to.

BELLE. You didn't even give me a chance!

MONTANA. Don't nobody GIVE you a chance in this man's world — you got to take it. Now, Charlie, you ain't told me what I need to know.

They talk aside.

RUBY. You poor kid! See, Montana ain't herself lately. She's worried about the miners going out on strike.

BELLE. But I walked three days to get here!

RUBY. You WALKED? Over them mountains? Where'd you sleep?

BELLE. Wherever I was. Say, you heard her say about taking a chance? Well, watch this. *Takes stage. To musicians.* Key of D, minor bridge, and you watch the time change.

      Harry enters, cleaned up, stares at Belle.
      She sees him. Sparks fly.

BELLE. *Sings, 'You Got to Go Out and Get It and Take Yourself Some.'*

  I dream of a house on top of a hill
  With two happy children, my Clarence and Phil.
  My husband adores more than my face,
  And I'm still a part of the whole human race.
    But this is a dream from a dime novelette,
    For sorrow is all that poor women will get:
    A husband who's broken and drowning in gin,
    And heartache from watching your babies grow thin.
  Oh, home, home on the range
  Is jumping from the frying pan into the fire.
  To all my friends of the gentle sex:
  Use your brains to save your necks.
  There's more to life than an early grave,
  But you must try, try, try, try —
  You got to go out and get it and take yourself some.
    'Cause Eve was a rebel, and she started it all
    When she took that fateful bite.
    And Sarah Bernhardt took a chance
    On that first opening night.
    Now what would have happened if Harriet Tubman
    Got off of that freedom train?
    And what would have happened if Joan of Arc
    Had thought she was insane?

Oh, home, home on the range
Is jumping from the skillet, down to the griddle,
Onto the skewer, around through the oven,
And into the fire.

MONTANA. Hold it!

Belle is terrified.

Climbs on stage. Take it from the middle of the A section.

MONTANA & BELLE. *Sing.*

If there's something you know how to do,
And your old man walks out on you,
Then your know-how will see you through.
But you must try, try, try, try —
You got to go out and get it and take yourself some,
Unless you want to leave it out there.

MONTANA.

And I ain't lyin'.

MONTANA & BELLE.

Unless you want to leave it out there.

BELLE.

It might get mildewed.

MONTANA & BELLE.

Unless you want to leave it out there.

RUBY.

I don't mean maybe.

MONTANA, BELLE & RUBY.

Unless you want to leave it out there!

MONTANA. Boys, I want to introduce you to my new singing sensation, Miss — what's your name, honey?

BELLE. Hortense — no, Belle! Belle Hayward. You mean — I got the job?

MONTANA. Sure do. Five dollars a week, sleep upstairs, meals at the bar.

BELLE. *In heaven.* Five dollars!

MONTANA. You came at the right time — looks like business is going to pick up. Ruby, get her some clothes so she won't have to sing behind a curtain. *Exits.*

HARRY. *Right there to help Belle offstage.* Belle, huh? Well, Belle is the right name for a lady makes such beautiful music. 'Go out and get it and take yourself some'!

RUBY. This here's Harry Potter, the hottest thing this side of Hades — he'll tell you.

BELLE. I can feel it.

Casey enters.

RUBY. And that's Casey.

Casey tips hat.

Watch out for him.

BELLE. Why? Is he a gunfighter?

RUBY. No — he's a socialist.

CASEY. Hello, Charlie.

SLADE. How's the Karl Marx of Colorado?

All laugh.

CASEY. Still working for a living. What's the word?

HARRY. Come on, Charlie — tell us how you gave 'em hell down in Denver!

SLADE. You boys seen the news? *Hands them paper.*

CASEY. Holy Toledo.

HARRY. God damn! Blew the son of a bitch clean out of the water! Them low-down, double-crossing Spaniards — that was nothing but cold-blooded murder!

CASEY. Murder? That was suicide, if it was them that did it.

RUBY. Whattaya mean 'if'?

Harry and Slade react likewise.

CASEY. Everybody knows the Spaniards are getting their asses kicked over in Cuba — why'd they want to come here and ask us for a war?

HARRY. Damn right, they asked for it — we ought to go in there and give it to 'em.

RUBY. We oughta make 'em remember the Maine!

All but Casey approve.

Not to mention all they done to them poor Cubans. You read it in the papers every day. Burning villages — herding people just like animals — killing innocent women and children.

CASEY. You might call it Spain's Indian War.

SLADE. God damn it, Casey — at a time like this show some respect for your country!

CASEY. Okay, Charlie — just tell us what happened at the meeting.

SLADE. Boys, I want to tell you. The company's got big city
lawyers working for them now.

CASEY. What did they say?

SLADE. Well, first, they said yes to the safety committee.

HARRY. They damn well better say yes!

SLADE. But they won't give the committee power to shut
down the mine.

Harry and Casey protest.

Now, they did not WANT to give us the eight-hour day.
This is where I was up against those smart lawyers I

28

mentioned. Well, it was a hard fight, but I outlasted them. Twelve hours underground might be all right for a rat, I said, but it's no life for a man. The boys want to see God's good sunshine, I told them. They want time — time to read a book, time to be with their children, time to be human beings! I don't mind telling you, when I finished there wasn't a dry eye in the room — nor a man who held out against the eight hours.

General rejoicing.

HARRY. What'd I tell you? This is my boy Charlie!

SLADE. At first, they were insisting on a one-third pay cut.

CASEY. So that's it.

RUBY. Those cheap meadow muffins!

HARRY. But you didn't fall for that, did you, Charlie?

SLADE. No. I talked them down — to 25 percent.

HARRY. That's their offer?

SLADE. That's the best we can get at this time.

CASEY. Well it ain't good enough.

HARRY. If the mines don't kill you, you starve to death!

CASEY. You call a meeting, Charles. We're going on strike.

Harry and Casey start off.

SLADE. That's what's wrong with radicals — they don't know how to change with the times. Do you know what the mine owners would say about us if we refused to produce vital war materiel?

CASEY. They'd say, 'We're losing millions — give 'em what they want.'

SLADE. If there's a war, we can get what we want peaceful-like. You just take it from old Charlie Slade — this war is going to be the best thing that ever happened to the American miner.

CASEY. The American mine owner, you mean.

HARRY. Hell, when they get more, we get more.

CASEY. Everything the capitalist gets he steals from us.

RUBY. *To Belle.* See what I mean? He reads foreign books.

29

CASEY. You want us to go over to Cuba and kick the Spaniards out?

SLADE. Damn right!

CASEY. We ought to be fighting right here, against the conquerors of the United States!

Slade starts for Casey.

HARRY. *Separates them.* Hell, we'll take the Spaniards on with one hand, and the mine owners with the other. Call a meeting, Charlie.

SLADE. You're crazy.

CASEY. And you had better invite the Mexicans to that meeting. 'Cause if you don't, I will. *Exits.*

RUBY. Oh, go read a book.

HARRY. Come on, everybody, let's celebrate!

SLADE. I got nothing to celebrate. *Exits.*

HARRY. Well, I do — America is going to show Spain who rules the ocean, the Copper City Miners' Union is going to show those mine owners who rules the Rockies, and I just met the most beautiful girl in the world! Come on, Ruby.

RUBY. *Takes stage.* All right, boys — let's have the 'Remember the Maine Rag.'

They dance. Ruby solos, Harry and Belle form chorus.

RUBY, HARRY & BELLE. *Sing 'The Remember the Maine Rag.'*

We'll be true to the red, white and blue

Our flag makes tyrants cringe.

They shrink from our might in our perilous fight

From Atlantic to Pacific rim.

So damn the torpedoes,

Full speed ahead is our fame.

We'll risk our necks for freedom's sake,

And always remember the Maine.

Alarm sounds. Montana enters.

BELLE. What's that?

MONTANA. Accident at the mine.

RUBY. There's more miners in the cemetery here than there is working.

Slade enters.

SLADE. Cave-in in Number 25! A Mexican was killed.

HARRY. At least it was no one we knew.

BELLE. A man's dead, still.

SLADE. If it was a Mexican, he probably brought it on himself.

MONTANA. I don't believe this! Seems to me Casey has a point. When you go on strike and the bosses offer your jobs to the Mexicans, you ain't given them one reason why they shouldn't take 'em. *Exits.*

HARRY. I'd like to see 'em try and take our jobs. We'd run 'em right on out of town. I tell you the white working man's being crowded out of this country, and we are the ones that made it. Damn companies already took away our land and our freedom — we don't need no Mexicans to come up in here and take away our jobs.

SLADE. I've told the boys a thousand times — you can't organize Mexicans.

Casey enters.

CASEY. The Mexicans just walked off the shift. They're holding a big meeting in the middle of town!

SLADE. Me and my big mouth.

HARRY. *To Belle.* I'll be back, pretty thing. Don't you go noplace.

BELLE. I'm staying — I got a job!

Exeunt men.

RUBY. Come on, honey, let's get you a costume. Harry's right — we don't have to worry none about the strike. Our business will be the last to suffer — miners drink the whole time they ain't working. They tell you it settles the dust. And if you don't mind a little friendly advice: they don't treat their women any better than they do them-selves.

Exeunt.

I.4

Maria's house, two days later. Mexican funeral procession: music, Mexican flag, banner: 'Sociedad Mutualista de los Mineros.' Tomás supports Maria. One by one mourners embrace Maria and depart, except one woman, who reverently sets the virgin on the table.

MOURNER.

Te acompaño en tus sentimientos, Maria.
Maria does not respond.
Some day we will all join Antonio in a better world.
MARIA. Antonio wanted a better world here.
Woman leaves. Maria looks at the virgin.
Belle enters, carrying dish, wears shawl over new dancehall costume.
BELLE. Mrs. Robledo?
MARIA. Sí?
BELLE. Do you speak English?
MARIA. When I have to.
BELLE. My name is Belle. I never been in a mine town before. Thought it was heaven — then the alarm bell rang, and I found out it's hell. I don't know what to say except I'm real sorry.
MARIA. Thank you, but your sympathy won't bring back my husband.
BELLE. Well — when a person's had a loss, I know it's hard to have to cook and all — so my boss, she made you this meat pie, and — here, you just take it and I'll go on and get out of your way.
MARIA. You ARE new here. White people don't help out Mexicans in this town. When my husband died, a white miner was working nearby. He didn't even try to lift the rocks off of him. He went to find another Mexicano. 'Hey,

32

Pancho — one of your boys had an accident.'
BELLE. I heard. That's terrible.
MARIA. A lot of terrible things have happened to us here —
this isn't even the worst! So take your food and go — I
can't eat white people's food!
BELLE. This ain't white people's food — it's black people's!
Where I come from, poor folks try to give each other a
hand. But if you're too high and mighty to need it, I know
plenty of folks that do. *To Tomás, who is entering.* Excuse
me. *Exits.*
MARIA. Señorita!
TOMÁS. Maria — ¿Que pasó?
MARIA. Nada.
TOMÁS. I have some good news.
      Maria gives him an unbelieving look.
Los gabachos are going on strike for the eight hour day.
MARIA. No.
TOMÁS. And they want us to go out with them.
MARIA. Now?
TOMÁS. Because we walked out, they think now's the right
time. Because they see that we're together, they want us to
support them.
      Maria shakes her head.
That guy Casey just came to see me. ¿Y sabes qué? Ellos
tienen miedo. They know we can take over their jobs.
MARIA. ¿Y qué le dijiste?
TOMÁS. Pues, I strung him along. 'Oh, sí — we'll have a
meeting and discuss your proposal.' That way we got
them off guard. They walk out and we walk in.
MARIA. *Carefully.* Be strikebreakers?
TOMÁS. Be miners! I mined copper ten years in Mexico —
diez años! Here, I move timber. And when some white
cowboy comes to work that's never been off his horse,
they put him over me as a driller and he makes a dollar a
day more than I do. Antonio died trying to keep estos

33

cabrones safe. And now he's going to be revenged.

MARIA. ¿Qué no, hombre? Take their jobs.

TOMÁS. We'll take their jobs, y mas. We'll take their houses. We're going to be the ones at the table, and they'll be outside looking in.

MARIA. Of course, you'll still be working twelve hours a day. But that won't matter — we'll be living like kings. Y tu sabes que los gabachos are going to try and stop you — but that's all right, the company will protect us. Then, when they put barbed wire and guards all around us, they're going to cut the wages — but we'll be happy, because we'll have paid back los gabachos.

TOMÁS. Bueno, we trust them.

MARIA. Eso. There's good white people.

TOMÁS. Sure — only I never met any. Mira. We walk out with them. Together, we win the strike. And then — ¡nos dan en la madre! They sell us out!

Casey enters.

CASEY. Señora Robledo?

MARIA. ¿Sí?

TOMÁS. Este es Casey.

CASEY. I knew your husband. I just came by to say if there's anything I can do, please feel free to ask.

TOMÁS. Gracias, Casey, but everything's taken care of.

Casey turns to go.

MARIA. Wait, Mr. Casey. There is one thing you can do for me. You can give me one reason why our people should join your strike.

CASEY. Is one reason enough?

MARIA. If it's good enough.

CASEY. Well — first, the man who was with your husband — he's been told to leave town. But the reason you should join the strike — that's easy. We need each other to win.

MARIA. It took you a long time to see that. But I know it's pride, stupid pride, to turn your back when somebody holds out their hand. *Clasps his hand.*

TOMÁS. Okay, Casey — I'll take a chance. It's time for our meeting. Come with me and make your proposal to the men. I'll translate and support you.

CASEY. Let's go!

They start off.

MARIA. *Putting on her shawl.* Shall we all go together?

Men are shocked.

TOMÁS. Maria? But there's only men there.

No response.

And what about Antonio?

MARIA. Antonio can't go, so I will. *Leads the way.*

Men shake their heads.

Exeunt.

II. 1

Railroad station in San Antonio, Texas,
Early Summer, 1898.
Washington Jefferson enters as hobo, with bundles.

LOUDSPEAKER.

Attention please, attention please. The Cross-Country Limited now loading on track 17 for Atchison, Topeka and Santa Fe. All aboard!
Woman enters.

NEWSVENDOR. Extry, extry, read all about it — Spanish fleet sunk in Vanilla. Extry!

JEFFERSON. Let me see a paper. *Offers no money.*

NEWSVENDOR. Four cent. Cost you money to read what the man doing now.

JEFFERSON. Never mind what he doing; just LEND me the part where it say if he got any jobs.

NEWSVENDOR. Jobs? Who gonna hire you?

JEFFERSON. Now, Granny. These rags are just a disguise. They conceal from an unfriendly world the true nature of Washington Jefferson, a scholar, a craftsman, a freedom fighter — and determined to resume the struggle for our people's liberation — just as soon as he gets a decent meal.

NEWSVENDOR. Nigger, please. I can't read, but I know what the Good Book say. I hear you young folks getting all excited, talking about Freedom Now — that black talk is gonna get you killed.

JEFFERSON. Shuffling for white folks ain't living.

NEWSVENDOR. No? Take a paper, son. *Gives him one.* Want ads in the middle, latest lynching on the back. Extry, extry, read all about it — Spanish fleet sunk in Vanilla. *Exits.*

JEFFERSON. *Reads.* 'Death and Destruction Wrought by Shot

36

and Shell.' Manila? Must be someplace in Cuba. 'The American victory is greeted joyfully by Fil-O-pino rebels' — Fil-O-pino? — 'who hail it as a great step toward their country's independence.'

LOUDSPEAKER. Attention please. The Capitol Express now arriving on Track 29, direct from Washington, DC.

Rough Rider Band enters, playing
'There'll Be a Hot Time in the Old Town Tonight.'
Washington Jefferson is blocking their path.

ROUGH RIDER 1. Get outta the way, boy. Go on, move!

JEFFERSON. It's your world. You mind if I live in it?

Theodore Roosevelt enters.

ROUGH RIDER 1. It's him!

ROUGH RIDER 2. Colonel Roosevelt!

ROUGH RIDER 3. Yippie!

They play.

ROOSEVELT. Men, this means a lot to me. And I want to say how proud I am to have command of this regiment formed of all western men. You're the men who won the West, who skinned the redskins, took the trimmings off Mexico — do you think you're a match for a bunch of undersized Dagoes?

ROUGH RIDER 1. We'll pick our teeth with 'em...

ROUGH RIDER 2. We'll hogtie 'em, drygulch 'em...

ALL 3. And send 'em to hell!

ROOSEVELT. By Jupiter, you men are chumps — I mean trumps! Looking to the days ahead, I have but one fear. I applaud Admiral Dewey for his victory in the Philippines — I applaud myself for having sent him there. But I'm afraid the war may not last till we get to Cuba!

ROUGH RIDER 1. That ain't fair!

ROUGH RIDER 2. We wanna fight!

ROUGH RIDER 3. We're ready!

ROOSEVELT. Therefore, we want to get through this training nonsense as quickly as possible and make haste to embark for Cuba on the first boat! So let's double-time it back to camp and get started. Detachment right face! Double-time! March!

Exeunt band.

By Jove — they've left me with my luggage! *Spies Jefferson.* Say, porter —

JEFFERSON. Say, Mr. Roosevelt!

ROOSEVELT. Thank you! *Steps down, but finding himself face-to-buttonhole with Jefferson, steps back up again quickly.*

JEFFERSON. How come the Republicans ain't kept the promises they made to the black man?

ROOSEVELT. Well now — these things take time.

JEFFERSON. We ain't got time! You talking 'bout starting a war down in Cuba, and you ain't done nothing for the black folks right here!

ROOSEVELT. *With elaborate secrecy.* The Cubans are black.

JEFFERSON. I ain't never read that in no paper.

ROOSEVELT. Let's face it — it wouldn't help sell the war if we advertised that the Cuban guerrillas are, nearly to a man, the descendants of Africans. Their ancestors were brought to the islands as slaves, just as your forebears were brought to these shores. Yes, my friend — by helping those patriots drive out the Spanish oppressor, America will be assisting the birth of a colored republic.

JEFFERSON. Now, that don't make sense.

ROOSEVELT. What's your name, my friend?

JEFFERSON. Washington Jefferson.

ROOSEVELT. And you're a porter?

JEFFERSON. I'm unemployed.

ROOSEVELT. An unemployed what?

JEFFERSON. Blacksmith, carpenter, baker, bricklayer and railroad fireman.

ROOSEVELT. Well, Jefferson — if I were a man of your race and capabilities, I would consider myself worse than a mollycoddle —

JEFFERSON. What's that?

ROOSEVELT. A coward! To be idling about here at home, while brave men are dying for black freedom in Cuba. I'd hear tom-toms, Jefferson. I'd feel the pounding blood, see the waving spears of my warrior ancestors. I would enlist today in the infantry and volunteer for service in Cuba.

JEFFERSON. I guess if freedom got a good start in Cuba, pretty soon it would just spread over here to the United States.

ROOSEVELT. I tell you, Jefferson — if the colored soldier fights bravely, he'll win freedom not only for the Cubans, but for his own people here at home — proving, by his courage and devotion, that he is ready to take his place as

our fellow-citizen. And earn 13 dollars a month, plus room and board.

JEFFERSON. Where would I go to sign up?

ROOSEVELT. There's a colored regiment training in Brownsville.

JEFFERSON. Thank you. *Picks up his bundles.*

ROOSEVELT. Private Jefferson.

JEFFERSON. *Salutes.* Yes, sir, Colonel Roosevelt, sir!

ROOSEVELT. Give me a hand with these bags.

Exeunt, Jefferson carrying luggage.

II.2

Montana's saloon, Copper City, six weeks later.
Belle enters, working; Harry, drinking, pursues her.

BELLE.

I told you I love you — now ain't that enough?

HARRY. If you love me, you ought to want to get married. It ain't natural for a woman not to want to get married.

BELLE. I'm just unnatural, I guess.

HARRY. You wasn't unnatural last night.

BELLE. And I ain't crazy this morning — but you are, drinking just when you're going to need what little sense you got. *Takes his glass.*

HARRY. I only drink 'cause I ain't never had nothing else.

BELLE. Give me a break.

HARRY. But if I had you — we'd get us a little house, pretty soon along come a couple of kids —

BELLE. Stop right there, Harry Potter! I seen every woman I know go down that road — and, mister, I ain't taking the first step.

Harry takes glass back.

Here you go promising me a rosy future, and I don't even know if you're going to live till tonight.

HARRY. I never know — every day I go to work. I ain't
scared now — the company's scared. Specially since that
old shaft house just blowed itself all over the mountain.

BELLE. I got a notion who helped it.

HARRY. I didn't say nothing about that. Now today, we're
going to show them they can't run no scabs up in here. I
tell you, girl, we're going to win this strike before we win
the war.

BELLE. It'll have to be soon, then — Spaniards give us Porto
Rico without even a fight.

HARRY. Anytime soon'll be too soon for me. I like spending
my time with you.

BELLE. You're forgetting that I have to work.

HARRY. Marry me and you won't have to.

BELLE. Oh, no — I could just stay home all day, cooking and
washing and scubbing the floors.

HARRY. At least they'd be your own floors, not some nigger
woman's.

BELLE. Harry Potter, don't you ever talk about Montana that
way to me! She's the best there is, and you know it.

HARRY. I know it — hell, it's just the way I talk.

BELLE. It's the way you think, and you ought to change it.
Montana takes a big risk every day she keeps this place
open. And I notice you don't talk about the Mexicans the
same way you used to.

HARRY. Well, they're doing all right, so far. That widow
woman, she really keeps them in line. Belle, it's hard to
change your thinking from the way that you was raised.
But if you was to marry me, you could keep me in line.

BELLE. Supposing I don't want the job?
                    He kisses her.
Harry, you're getting under my skin.
                Deputy enters, spits for attention.

HARRY. It's the law. Don't you serve him.

BELLE. Montana says we serve whoever comes in, and she

don't want no trouble. *To deputy.* What can I do for you?

DEPUTY. A little of what you was doing for him would be fine.

BELLE. What he gets ain't on our menu. But can I offer you a kick in the pants, or a fat lip?

DEPUTY. Where's the boss?

BELLE. The boss is out. What do you want?

DEPUTY. I want you to tell Montana that the boys around here cleaned the Indians out of this country, and they want to keep it one hundred percent American. So it ain't very smart for a nigger woman who's got her whole fortune tied up in mirrors and glassware — *tosses a glass* — to let her place turn into the headquarters of a bunch of anarchistic, greaser-loving, dynamiting traitors, who'd go on strike while their country's at war.

HARRY. *Approaches him.* Well, now. That there is a real pretty badge you have on.

DEPUTY. You like it?

Both finger holsters.

HARRY. I'd like to have one — for my dog.

As both start to draw, Montana enters,
blasting with shotgun.

That's my girl Montana!

MONTANA. *To Deputy.* Get out.

DEPUTY. I'm going — but the sheriff'll be back to shut you down for good. *Exits.*

MONTANA. I just beat him to it. I'm closing till the end of the strike.

HARRY. You can't do that, Montana — this place means too much to the boys.

MONTANA. There's other bars.

HARRY. Can't stand the heat, huh? I don't even want to see you, Montana. I never took you for a scab.

BELLE. Wait —

HARRY. I'll see YOU at the station. *Exits.*

BELLE. I never took you for one who'd turn her back on her friends.

MONTANA. I don't have friends. Only customers.

BELLE. You won't have customers after the strike if you close down now.

MONTANA. And if I stay open, I won't have a place.

BELLE. The miners ain't going to let the company kick you out — Harry told me. They're making 'Amnesty for Montana' one of their demands.

MONTANA. You being in love don't mean there's stars in my eyes. You ain't seen a lot of strikes where you come from. You think all they got to do is walk out, and the bosses will come crawling on their hands and knees to give them what they want. Do you know there's a trainload of strike-breakers coming?

BELLE. Sure, and I know the union's going to stop them.

MONTANA. How can they, when there's an army of deputies guarding them? Tomorrow the mines will reopen with scabs. The company can afford the extra expense, but how long can the miners hold out without wages? They'll start sneaking back, one man at a time. Because it's human nature — everybody takes care of Number One.

BELLE. I got to hand it to you, Montana. You sure know how to do that.

MONTANA. I ought to — ain't nobody taken care of me since my mama, and I was sold away from her when I was ten years old. I have shook my ass and sang out my heart in every boomtown from Comstock to Coeur d'Alene, and I'm tired. And now you stand there, young, blonde and beautiful, with a man outside begging to marry you, and you're asking me to give up my last stand for a bunch of Mexican and white miners, and I don't even know which one will sell out the other first.

BELLE. There you go again, dragging in color where it don't belong. You sound just like that Mexican woman.

43

MONTANA. There's a job for you when I reopen if you want
it.
BELLE. I don't. *Going.* Goodbye, Montana. I won't never
forget what you done for me. *Exits.*
MONTANA. *Sings, 'Song of the Person Caught in the Middle.'*
    Hey, don't you think the world's a great place?
    Hey, don't you think that paying your dues pays off?
    Hey, look at me: worked hard all my life.
    Stayed inside the law — and now I'm on top!
      And now I get to be myself
      To stand up and fight for the right thing.
      When some hard-working man is robbed of his bread,
      You stick your neck out and yell 'Stop, thief!'
Spoken. Oh, yeah — you can be brave. But watch out.
The rewards of honest work make you fearful. It's better
To look the other way, take care of your own.
Sings.
    Hey, don't you think the world's a great place?
    Hey, don't you think that paying your dues pays off?
    Hey, look at me: worked hard all my life.
    Stayed inside the law — and now I'm on top!
      And now I get to be myself,
      A person with something to share,
      To make the world warm for someone who's cold —
      It's sweet to have folks you can care for.
Spoken. Oh, yeah, you can be generous. But watch out.
The rewards of honest work can be pretty damn stingy.
On a cold winter's night, if someone asks to share your
    coat —
Forget it! Because the choice is a question.
Of whether one, or both of you, will freeze.
Sings.
    Lord, what's a person to do now?
    I got something to lose now.
    The powers that be decide the rules:

The deck is stacked, the people will lose.
And there's nothing new under the sun.
We're all under that same thumb.
And I guess the price of courage
Is more than I can afford.
    Maria enters with pan and spoon, sets them on bar.
MARIA. I'd like a whiskey. *Holds out money.*
    Montana takes money and serves her, eyeing her all the time.
Nice day.
MONTANA. For somebody.
MARIA. Nice place.
MONTANA. I like it.
MARIA. *Tosses down the whiskey, nearly chokes.* Nice —
    whiskey.
MONTANA. Who are you?
MARIA. My name is Maria.
MONTANA. You the one wouldn't eat the food.
MARIA. That's right.
MONTANA. You best of friends with the white folks now.
MARIA. We're fighting on the same side.
MONTANA. And you come here to tell me I'm siding with the
    company.
    Maria does not deny this.
Well, look here. You ain't got no call to be telling me
nothing. Your people ain't never been in here.
MARIA. My people didn't used to get along with your cus-
    tomers. Now it's 'Come on over to Montana's.' I wanted
    to see what made this place so special. *Walks around, shrugs.*
    Whatever it was, I guess it's gone now.
MONTANA. It ain't gone — you looking right at it.
MARIA. The lady who'd rather sing for strikebreakers?
    Offstage many pots and pans start clanking in time.
MONTANA. What's that?
MARIA. It's all the women. We got the wives, we got the
    schoolteachers, we even got the women from Division

45

Street. We're marching down to the train station in front of the men — we're going to meet those scabs with beautiful music. *Bangs her pan and spoon to offstage noise.* It's not too late for you to come with us.

MONTANA. God damn. *Takes a gun from the bar.* Señora, let's go.

Exeunt.

II.3

The train station.
Maria, Montana, Belle, Ruby, a Mexican woman enter,
clanking pots and pans, form a line facing out.

MARIA.

The women came from all over town.
The funeral train pulled into the station.
The scabs were riding packed on the flatcars, like freight.
Hungry men and mean men, and some who didn't know no better.
Riding every car, there was a chain of armed guards.
Pots and pans and war whoops.
When the concert stopped, we all began shouting.

ALL. Scabs go home! Scabs go home!

MARIA. The scabs looked out from behind the deputies.
Saw five hundred women, looking mighty mad.
Song-chant.

MONTANA. Will you take your brother's job?

ALL. Don't get off that train.

WOMAN. Are you a man or a yellow dog?

ALL. Don't get off that train.

RUBY. Injure one and you injure all.

ALL. Don't get off that train.

BELLE. Together we win, divided we fall.

ALL. Don't get off that train.

MARIA. One scab said,
MONTANA.   'I don't like it.'
MARIA. One said,
WOMAN.   'Let's go back to Denver.'
MARIA. The deputies yelled 'All men off' and pushed them
   off the train.
BELLE. 'Are you afraid of a bunch of women?'
MARIA. That's when the women tore into the scabs.
      Whooping and clanking, women rush forward.
   'You women leave them men alone or we'll be forced to
      shoot you.
   Now go on home and let us through. These men are going
      to work.'

When we didn't get back, they aimed their rifles.
Then, from behind the station, marched a thousand loving
    miners.

> *Men enter, aiming rifles. All chant softly*
> *under what follows: 'Get back on that train.'*

CASEY. When the strikebreakers saw us, they ran crawling,
    falling backwards.
When the deputies saw us, they lowered their guns.
When the engineer saw us, he blew the whistle.
Whistle.
And all the scavengers jumped back on the train.
And because our town is at the end of a canyon —

MEN. Yeah?

CASEY. And seeing as that crew was in a bit of a hurry —

MEN. Yeah?

CASEY. That old Yellow Dog Special backed up all the way to Denver!

ALL. Ya —

MARIA. With the passengers discussing the lesson they had learned.

ALL. —hoo!

All rejoice.

MONTANA. Come on, everybody, let's celebrate! You know Montana's place is always open!

II.4

Montana's, immediately following.
Miners and women make ready to celebrate.

HARRY.

Hold on now, everybody. Before we all swing our partners, I'd like to say a few words. See, I learned a big lesson here today, and that is that all the miners, and all the women, are brothers and sisters — and it don't matter what color.
Applause.
Now, I didn't always think this way.

TOMÁS. De veras.

HARRY. But today we marched together. And it felt good!
Applause.
So I want to hear it for unity!

ALL. Unity! Unidad! *They drink to it. All dance.*

TOMÁS. ¡Compañeros y compañeras! I also would like to say a few words. There's going to be hard days in front of us. We're going to be cold, and we're going to be hungry. Pero....

RUBY. *Interrupts him.* But right now we want to celebrate! *Applause. Music starts. The people perform for each other. Belle and Harry dance a hillbilly shuffle; Maria and Tomás a bamba; Montana a cakewalk. Finally, by popular demand, Ruby and Casey shake hands, then do an Irish jig. All exit dancing and singing 'Solidarity Forever.' Slade enters.*

SLADE. Harry! Casey! *Sees that they are gone.* To hell with them. They're so excited about their damn strike, they didn't hear the GOOD news: Spain has surrendered! Cuba is free — and it's ours. *He announces intermission, exits.*

III. 1

A cantina, San Juan, Puerto Rico, early in 1899.
Music. Bar lady enters, sets up bar.
Musician enters.

¡Hola!   MUSICIAN.

BAR LADY. ¿Gusta un trago? *Pours him a drink.*
Man and Maritza enter with picket signs:
'Abajo con United Fruit,' 'Que viva la huelga,'
'Jornada de 8 horas.'

MAN & MARITZA. ¡Viva Puerto Rico Libre! ¡Que viva!
Musician plays.

ALL. *Dance, sing 'Va Terminar.'*
Llegaron con promesas
pretendiendo sinceridad,

se robaron las riquezas y tomaron libertad.
Nos ofrecieron su 'progreso'
impresionando la juventud,
pero el costo fue de ingresos, manteniendo esclavitud.
No, no, no — esa infamia va terminar.
No, no, no — esa infamia va terminar.
*Washington Jefferson enters in U.S. Army uniform
with corporal's stripes, flower stuck in rifle barrel.
Music dies.*
BAR LADY. Mira, mira quién llegó — ¡un yanqui fumado! Un soldado norte-americano. *To Jefferson.* ¿Qué quiere? ¿Eh? ¿Eh? ¿Qué quiere?
JEFFERSON. El drinko.
BAR LADY. *Pours him one.* Salud.
JEFFERSON. 'Salud!' *Salutes. Raises his glass.* To freedom!
*He drinks; all watch him sarcastically.
He gives Maritza the eye, matches his skin against hers.*
El same-o! *Gives her the flower.*
MUSICIAN. Oh-oh — Maritza!
Jefferson signals Musician to play.
MARITZA. ¡Música! ¡Música!
MAN. ¿Vas a bailar con el?
MARITZA. ¡Sí!
JEFFERSON. Play that funky music, white boy. *Gives him money.*
*Musician resumes the tune. Jefferson and Maritza dance.
He starts out doing cakewalk, but learns her style. Finally,
they dance together.*
OTHERS. *Sing.*

Compraron a gobernantes
establecieron la burguesia
mantienen su poder con los lacayos y policia.
La gente de los campos,
de pueblos y ciudad,
todos juntos en la lucha vam' obtener la libertad.

No, no, no — esa infamia va terminar.
No, no, no — esa infamia va terminar.
No, no, no — el imperialismo se va acabar.
No, no, no — esa infamia va terminar.
    Va terminar. *Four times, with inspiración.*
No, no, no — ¡esa infamia va terminar!

MUSICIAN. Maritza, José — vamos a la manifestación. ¡Es muy tarde!

MAN. *Picks up his sign.* ¡Maritza! ¡Vamos!

MARITZA. Momento, momento.

MAN. Él puede bailar, pero eso no le quite que es un yanqui fumado.

    Exeunt man and musician.

MARITZA. ¡Ahora te veo!

JEFFERSON. Uh...vio, crio...mamacita, and things. *Whips out Army phrase book, searches.*

    Bar lady fumes in background during what follows.

Reads. 'Yo soy un amigo de Usted.'

MARITZA. *Reads.* 'I am your friend.'

JEFFERSON. Uh HUH! *Searches, reads.* 'Puerto Rico es un país muy linda.'

MARITZA. *Reads.* 'Puerto Rico is a beautiful country.'

JEFFERSON. Right! *Searches, reads.* 'Los Estados Unidos es un amigo de Puerto Rico.'

MARITZA. *Reads.* 'The United States is Puerto Rico's friend'?

JEFFERSON. Right!

MARITZA. *Not reading.* Wrong!

JEFFERSON. You speak English!

MARITZA. I learn. We all have to learn.

JEFFERSON. Well, lick my leg and call me Lollipop. Sometimes it's too easy to find a woman down here, but you the first one I can talk to. Which is a pity and a shame, because the boy being shipped to the Philippines tomorrow. But we can make the most of it — what's your name?

MARITZA. Maritza.

JEFFERSON. Me llamo Washington.

MARITZA. Like the president. We have to learn that, too.

JEFFERSON. You doing fine. Mighty fine. You know, I like Porto Rico. 'Course it's still kinda funky, with all them chickens and scroungy horses all over the street, but when we gets it fixed up it going to be a right nice place. Like y'all music, too. *Hums the song.* What the words mean?

MARITZA. *Sings.*

They came with their promises
Pretending sincerity,
But they robbed us of our riches and they took our
    liberty.
They offered us their progress,
Impressing all our youth,
But the cost was our dependence and our credit's
    overdue.
No, no, no — this oppression's going to end.
No, no, no — this oppression's going to end.

JEFFERSON. *Knowing the answer.* Who 'they'?

MARITZA. You.

JEFFERSON. Americans, huh? This ain't the first time I heard it. Little kids running up and down the street yelling 'Yanqui go home!' You people got to be the cold-heartedest, ungratefullest pack of thieves in all of God's creation. I got shot at for y'all! My partner done died for your freedom!

MARITZA. He should have stayed home.

JEFFERSON. He sure as hell should have. And where would y'all be? You didn't have nothing when we got here!

MARITZA. No United Fruit Company — no laws against going on strike!

BAR LADY. ¿Qué dice? ¿Qué dice?

MARITZA. Dice que antes no teníamos nada.

BAR LADY. ¿Sí? Dile eso: que antes teníamos de todo, y ahora se lo robaron todo! ¡Y quieren transformar la isla a una fabrica! ¡Dile eso! ¡Dile! ¡Dile!

Maritza starts to translate.

JEFFERSON. Don't let her be putting words in your mouth! That's another thing — races all mixed up down here. I seen you dancing with that white boy.

MARITZA. North Americans are black and white — we're Puerto Ricans! That's what I no understand. Why you fight for a country where you have no rights?

JEFFERSON. I'm fighting for my rights. Me being a soldier down here means a better life for my people back home.

MARITZA. But my people pay!

Shouts, gunshots offstage.
White lieutenant enters.

LIEUTENANT. Hey, corporal! We got a god damn riot on our hands! On the double!

Jefferson grabs rifle. Jefferson and lieutenant exeunt.

BAR LADY. ¡Maritza, vamonos! ¡Están matando a los manifestantes! *Exeunt.*

Jefferson and lieutenant enter,
marching musician and man at gunpoint.

Bar lady and Maritza enter.

MAN. ¿Qué importa la cara, compañera?

Jefferson hesitates.

LIEUTENANT. I said march 'em, not take 'em for a walk —
   move!

Jefferson shoves musician: he falls. Maritza helps him up.

JEFFERSON. Listen, mama — I'm just doing a job here, I —

MARITZA. Yanqui go home!

LIEUTENANT. I said move!

Exeunt men.

Maritza is still holding flower. She throws it down, exits.

III.2

Washington, DC, early in 1899.
Roosevelt enters.

ROOSEVELT.

Bow Asia — South America, subside.
And Europe, make way for the new contender.
   We're young, rough, ready, with but one weak point:
   Our President, as soft as an eclair.
   The bout with Spain — that splendid little war —
   Won us an island empire: now McKinley
   Loses his nerve, and fails to grasp the prize.
   But all's not lost: I'm here. I have a plan.

Displays bullhorn, then hides.
McKinley enters.

MCKINLEY. Now empire has brought forth prosperity.
   But conscience groans.
   Each night, I walk this floor and pray for guidance.
   Each night, silence replies.

ROOSEVELT. *Offstage, using God's voice.* WILLIAM MCKINLEY?

MCKINLEY. Who's that?

ROOSEVELT. YOU DARE TO ASK?

MCKINLEY. No, no!

ROOSEVELT. YOU BLEW IT, TURKEY.

MCKINLEY. I gave up Cuba!

> *Silence.*

> Take back Puerto Rico!

> *Silence.*

You can HAVE the Philippines!

ROOSEVELT. KEEP THE ISLANDS!

MCKINLEY. It's all right? What about the Filipinos?

ROOSEVELT. WHAT ABOUT THEM?

MCKINLEY. They believe us allies! Is it Christian
  To overrun a peaceful, trusting people?

ROOSEVELT. YES, IT IS YOUR DUTY TO UPLIFT
  AND CIVILIZE, BY ANY MEANS, YOUR SMALL
  BROWN BROTHER. GO, AND SIN NO MORE.

MCKINLEY. Did he say 'any means'?

> *Roosevelt enters.*

ROOSEVELT.   No answer yet?

MCKINLEY. He spoke.
  I must preach everywhere this simple message:

58

The Filipino is a savage creature,
Much like the Indian. Self-government
Is for the Anglo-Saxon, who brings peace.
Go, give the Army orders to attack.

MORGAN. *Offstage.* HOLD ON A GOD–DAMN MINUTE.
Roosevelt looks behind curtain. Morgan enters.
Sorry to interrupt your bedtime story.
Fired up to pacify the Philippines?

MCKINLEY. That is my only calling.

ROOSEVELT. Those fair isles will be saved from beastly
darkness,
If it takes every fighting man we've got.

MORGAN. 'Your only calling'? 'Every fighting man'?
Meanwhile, at home we're threatened with rebellion.

ROOSEVELT & MCKINLEY. Rebellion?

MORGAN.   Labor agitation.
Get it? The Rocky Mountains blaze with strikes.

ROOSEVELT. Those flames could spread.

MORGAN. Myself and Rockefeller formed a trust:
Amalgamated Copper. We bought mines
With ores worth millions, in the western states.
Those mines are shut.

MCKINLEY.   How foul.

MORGAN.   I want them open.

MCKINLEY. Immediately! Have you tried negotiations?

ROOSEVELT. Rot! Anarchists and workers understand
One argument: a blast from your revolver.

MORGAN. I like the way he thinks.

MCKINLEY. Wait, now, gentlemen. I'd planned
To campaign next year as a friend of labor —

MORGAN. Campaigns cost money.

MCKINLEY.   Hark, I hear His voice.
'To close the mines, in time of war, is treason.
'Let punishment be swift.' *To Roosevelt.* You have your
orders. *Exits.*

MORGAN. A man will generally have two reasons for what he does:

A good one, and the real one.

ROOSEVELT.   That's a good one.

MORGAN. At home, abroad, we triumph by one trick:

ROOSEVELT. Make promises, but carry a big stick.

Exeunt.

III.3

Copper City, a few weeks later. A street.
Tomás, Harry enter from hunting, with game in bag.

HARRY.

Come down the crick, he couldn't have been fifty yards from me. Still as an Indian — biggest old buck I ever saw. Had a eight-point rack, must have been four foot across. I had a clear shot, too — I don't know what spooked him.

TOMÁS. He smelled you, man. You better take a bath.

HARRY. In this weather? Damn! If I'd have got him, the whole town been eating venison.

TOMÁS. That deer was skinny as we are.

HARRY. Well, these squirrels is fat. That was some shooting, hey Thomas? Just give me a bag of beans, a fire, and a few rounds for my rifle — we could stay out another whole winter.

TOMÁS. You and me could. It's harder on men that got kids.

HARRY. You ain't seen a kid eats like my wife's little brother.

TOMÁS. Listen, Harry. I got to talk to you about the union.

Slade enters.

SLADE. Howdy, boys — you been hunting?

HARRY. No, we been swimming.

SLADE. You boys are the salt of the earth. Out at dawn in the dead of winter, hunting meat for the union soup kitchen. It's too bad we don't have more boys who would give this fight all they got.

TOMÁS. We got 200 Mexicanos, Slade, that ain't never going to quit.

HARRY. And 500 white miners, that will outlast any Mexicans.

SLADE. Spoken like fighters. That's the true union spirit, that shines forth from the brightest pages in the history of labor. Like the great Pullman strike, back in '94. A hundred and twenty-five thousand trainmen went out. They shut down twenty railroads. They held the country in a tight grip.

TOMÁS. ¡Eso!

HARRY. You know damn well they won!

SLADE. No, they lost. The owners combined. The men were driven back to work by the United States Army. Against a small outfit like this here, you got a chance. Keep up the good work, boys. I'll see you at the meeting tomorrow. We got some decisions to make. *Exits.*

TOMÁS. That vendido's going to try and call off the strike.

HARRY. Maybe he knows something we don't know.

TOMÁS. He knows how to look out for himself.

HARRY. He won't get nobody to listen to him. Everybody knows the son of a bitch ain't worth the tinfoil on his big fat cigars.

TOMÁS. That's why my people want to elect a new president.

HARRY. Your people don't waste a lot of time, do they? Who's the Mexican candidate, you?

TOMÁS. We know your people ain't ready for that. We're proposing Casey. We need you to support us.

HARRY. I'll vote for the man.

TOMÁS. ¡Ándale, 'mano!

HARRY. But not for his ideas. Casey don't really care if we win this strike. All he wants is for the working people to take over the country.

TOMÁS. And we are going to start here!

Exeunt.

61

III.4

Montana's, a short time later. The bar is now a
cooperative store. Maria enters with broom and sweeps.
Belle sets up counter but is distracted by newspaper;
Montana hangs red banner: 'United We Win —
8 Hour Day, Equal Pay, Safety,' in English and Spanish,
with union insignia.

MARIA.

That banner still looks good.

BELLE. I'm glad something does. *Back to paper.* My God,
more atrocities in the Philippines. 'Luzon Rebels Torture,
Kill American Soldiers.' Lordy, them Filipinos are worse
than the Indians.
        Montana and Maria exchange a look.
MONTANA. How's that — neither one want to give up their
country?
BELLE. Listen to this! 'Business Booms, Country Rides on
Wave of Prosperity.' I wish that old wave would just roll
right in here.
MONTANA. *To Maria.* You and Casey got a plan for this
meeting?
MARIA. Sí, señora.
BELLE. *Overhears.* Her and Casey got a lot more than that.
MONTANA. He's the perfect man for you — every way but
one.
MARIA. Things have changed here. I see the person, not the
color.
        Sarah enters with shopping bag.
SARAH. Howdy, ladies.
        They greet her.
Give me a quarter pound of lard, a pound of flour and a
half pound of beans.

BELLE. We been out of lard for a week.

SARAH. No lard? *As Maria bends to fill her order, Sarah checks to see she's not watched, steals a potato from sack on counter.*

MARIA. Here's the flour. Now the frijoles...

Sarah steals another potato.

This time Maria sees. She catches Sarah's wrist.

So others can't hear. Put it back.

SARAH. Take your greasy hand off me.

MARIA. *Slams Sarah's hand on counter.* She was stealing potatoes.

MONTANA. It's been a long winter.

BELLE. You apologize to Maria! Look at her! Stealing from the Co-op. This food is what keeps the strike going!

SARAH. To hell with the strike! Everybody knows you all help yourselves.

BELLE. You're a liar! *Lunges for Sarah.*

Montana holds Belle back.

SARAH. And you don't have families! You ain't scrimping and straining to feed a husband and babies on fifty cents a day strike benefits!

MARIA. No, because we don't get that much.

SARAH. Well, there'd be a little more for everybody if all them Mexicans wasn't getting extra 'cause they got too many kids!

MARIA. Pay for what you got and get out of here.

SARAH. *Pays.* This don't leave me nothing for coal. I suppose you're gonna report me to the meeting. Go ahead — because there's plenty of folks that's as fed up as I am. And we are just about finished letting a bunch of radicals tell us what to do. *Exits.*

BELLE. Ooh!

MARIA. I wish you still had some whiskey.

BELLE. You think there's really lots like her?

MONTANA. Not in this town.

Ruby enters with suitcase.

63

RUBY. Montana? I was going to sneak away without saying nothing, but when the time came I just couldn't do it. I hate leaving, but I ain't used to living like this. Besides, I got to think of the future — you know I ain't getting any younger. So, I'm off to Frisco — gonna make it in the Big Time.

BELLE. I bet you will, too.

RUBY. Oh, Belle — I wish you was coming with me! But she had to go and get married. I done what I could for her all the same: taught her all the steps I know, 'cept my secret ones. Here — my silver tap shoes. I want you to have 'em.

BELLE. Thank you, Ruby.

RUBY. They always was a little too big, anyway. And Maria

— my gold cross with the ruby on it.

MARIA. Oh, no — you keep it.

RUBY. Use it when you pray for me. Montana — you been just like a mother to me.

MONTANA. If I was your mama, I would whup your ass.

RUBY. You don't need me. You're all so brave — I know you'll win, someday.

Train whistle.

Well, it's train time. You tell the boys my last words was wishin' them luck. *Exits.*

BELLE. *Running after her.* Goodbye, Ruby!

MARIA. My neighbors left last night. Didn't say a word. In the morning — just gone.

The meeting is about to start.
Tomás, Harry, Casey, a white miner,
Davey (Belle's brother) drift in.

MINER. Where's Charlie? It's time for the meeting.

Harry kisses Belle. Maria takes Casey aside.

MARIA. There's a whole lot of people going to listen to Charlie! You got to take the lead now or we could lose the strike!

CASEY. Ain't I ever told you — you can't lose a strike.

Slade enters, takes place and gavels: all take places.

SLADE. Before I call this meeting to order — ladies, this isn't a town meeting like we been having: this is a regular business meeting of Local #27, so, while nobody loves you womenfolk more than I do, I got to ask you to clear out.

MINER. No petticoats allowed!

Women, Casey, Tomás, Harry protest.

That's a bunch of mule pucky — it's my job!

MONTANA. It's my bar!

HARRY. *To Slade.* You can't do that!

SLADE. I want to remind you boys that this meeting will be conducted according to Robert's Rules of Order.

BELLE. Robert who?

TOMÁS. Mr. Chairman. It's not just Local #27 on strike — it's this whole town! And this meeting is going to decide the future of the strike, so las compañeras have a right to be here!

MINER. Boo!

Others agree loudly with Tomás.

SLADE. The chair is overruled. I was only trying to spare the ladies' tender feelings, because what I got to say ain't going to be easy to listen to.

Women resent this.

BELLE. We're ready.

SLADE. Brothers and sisters, we have been on strike for almost a year.

MONTANA. Is that what you called us here to tell us?

Women, Casey, Tomás, Harry laugh.

SLADE. I called this meeting to tell you WHY they let us stay out so long. Because our mine was being sold to the Amalgamated Copper Company.

This is news to all.

Casey, Tomás, Harry appreciate its significance.

Others ask, 'Amalgamated What?' 'What's that?' etc.

HARRY. The copper trust.

SLADE. The Amalgamated Copper Company was only formed last year, but already it is the biggest mining trust in the world. It owns hundreds of mines: here, Mexico, Chile — and now I read where it's staking claims in the Philippines.

CASEY. Proving that this war is the best thing that ever happened to the American miner.

SLADE. This is a company that can last out a strike. We're not just up against some smart lawyers — we're up against Morgan and Rockefeller! Brothers and sisters, as your president, I don't think we can beat them.

This hits people hard.

CASEY. So you want to join them?

MINER. You can't beat J. P. Morgan!

MARIA. We have to!

TOMÁS. You shouldn't be president if you want us to go back. I say, abajo con Amalgamated — they're bigger, that just means we fight harder!

Montana, Maria, Belle, Casey agree. Harry is silent.

Sabes qué, Slade — you ain't never given us the leadership we needed on this strike! I move we hold an election!

MARIA. Right now!

This creates a sensation.
Montana, Maria, Belle and Casey argue
with miner.

SLADE. The brother has made a very significant motion, a motion that we should all think about very seriously.

MONTANA. Damn right!

SLADE. But right now it's out of order, because there is another matter on the floor.

Tomás, Montana, Maria, Belle, Casey protest.

Gavels. Brothers and sisters, I did not make the suggestion I did with the thought that it was going to make me popular.

Sarah enters, breathless, starts to speak, stops.

But I had an experience on the way over here that made me determined to speak out at this meeting. I encountered a grieving family, following a tiny coffin.

All are visibly moved.

I knelt to comfort their little girl. She said, 'My daddy's on strike, and we run out of coal, so my baby brother died of pneumonia.' Do we want to see more babies dying?

CASEY. Do we want to see more babies growing up in slavery?

SARAH. Well, there's going to be more pneumonia, because the Amalgamated Copper Company has cut off our coal! The station agent told me. The railroad got an order — no more coal comes in.

This is a bombshell. All talk at once.

Now do you believe it's time to quit?

MONTANA. Look like some folks thought this strike was
going to be a picnic. Come time they find out it ain't, they
want to tuck in their tail and go running for shelter!

SLADE. Brothers and sisters, you have all fought, and fought
valiantly. You have a lot to be proud of. If you go back
now you will not have been beaten.

TOMÁS. No — we will have surrendered!

HARRY. If we stay out, we could lose everything!

TOMÁS. It's one thing for you to go back on the old terms —
you was making a dollar a day more than we was!

HARRY. So if you don't get that stinking dollar, the rest of us
got to starve?

Everybody argues with his or her neighbor.

Maria and Casey confer.

BELLE. Harry, have you gone crazy?

HARRY. Can you beat J. P. Morgan?

SLADE. I'd like to call the question.

MARIA. Mr. Chairman! Point of order! You have left out the most important item on the agenda. We always read the list of contributors to our strike fund at the beginning of every meeting.

TOMÁS. That's right!

SLADE. I thought we could waive that, seeing as —

CASEY. Read it!

MONTANA. Let's hear from the people!

MARIA. Fifty cents a day seems like a very small benefit, until we remember where it came from. This week, the Butte Miners' Union gave us $1000.

Stunned silence, followed by Ohs and Ahs.

BELLE. Butte is okay.

MARIA. Coeur d'Alene, $700.

Applause.

Victor — that's a small town — $50.

TOMÁS. Let's hear it for Victor!

Cheers.

MARIA. Morenci, Arizona — y estos son mexicanos — $500!

DAVEY. Miners are okay!

Cheers and applause.

CASEY. *Signals for quiet.* These are all our fellow workers who are giving us money out of their own pockets so we can stay out on strike. Now the question is, why are they doing this? Is it some kind of Christian charity?

TOMÁS. Hell, no.

CASEY. That's right; it's something better than that — it's class solidarity. Those miners know that we are fighting for them. Now what's the big lesson we learned here today?

BELLE. That we ain't going to have no more coal.

CASEY. That's right; Amalgamated Copper is trying to make it cold for us — which only proves that we are making things too hot for them.
> *All take note. This is a new view.*

Today we learned that to us unworthy vessels, here in Copper City, has fallen a great honor: we're fighting the first battle against the copper trust. We're standing practically on the edge of a new century, and our battle here is part of a great war that is going to decide whether the many that produce the wealth, or the few that steal it— *looks at Slade* — are going to control the future of this country.

SARAH. Mr. Casey, you could talk the angels out of their wings.

SLADE. Shut up, woman — you're out of order!

CASEY. Mr. Chairman, I call the question.

SLADE. All right — all those in favor of going back to work.
> *Only he and miner are in favor.*

Glares at Harry. Opposed?
> *All others raise their hands, but Harry does so slowly.*

The motion dies.
> *Tomás, Montana, Maria, Belle cheer.*

You people think the revolution's starting next week. I won't answer for what happens now.
> *General rejoicing.*

MONTANA. Quiet down now. We got a surprise.
> *Belle, Maria, Montana move upstage.*

MARIA. Los quiero presentar: las mujeres de Copper City.
> *They bow.*

This corrido was written in Bisbee, Arizona, about our strike — and it's being sung at every stop along the Santa Fe Railroad!

MARIA, BELLE & MONTANA. *Sing, 'El Corrido de Copper City.'*
> En el invierno de la noventa y nueve
> en un pueblito por ay en Colorado

70

toda la gente haciendo sacrificios
que los mineros salieron del trabajo.
En las demandas pidieron ocho horas
y que la pagen igual al Méxicano
pero el patron que manda no le importa
mando esquiroles y mucho diputado.
¡Viva la huelga! The strike in Copper City
que todo el mundo está por apoyar.
aunque les manden un tren de esquiroles
la gente es firme — los van a rechazar.

MARIA.

Todo el mundo espera el resultado
de los huelgistas allá en Colorado
hasta los perros ya ladran enredados
¡tomando whiskey pa' estar calentados!

BELLE & MONTANA.

The whites and Mexicans would not be divided
And now the bosses hope winter will defeat them.
But it takes more than wind and snow to stop the
    people —
They're making plenty of good moonshine to heat them!

ALL THREE.

¡Viva la huelga! The strike in Copper City
que todo el mundo esta por apoyar.
¡Viva la huelga! The strike in Copper City,
que todo el pueblo unido va triunfar!

Applause, cheers. Casey takes gavel and pounds for order.

TOMÁS. I made a motion before. We want to hold an
election.

CASEY. Just a minute, Tomás, I think I still have the floor.
Brothers and sisters, I'm really proud that we decided to
stay out and fight.

Crowd agrees.

And now, I would like to introduce a resolution.

All listen expectantly.

71

'Resolved: no worker who does not wish to betray his class should enlist for military service against the Filipinos who are struggling for their independence.'

Good-natured groans.

BELLE. Oh, for God's sake!

CASEY. Hold on — I'm not asking you to pass on my pretty words: I'm asking you to decide a man's fate. Davey?

DAVEY. *Steps forward.* Howdy, folks. Some of you know me — I'm Harry Potter's brother-in-law.

BELLE. Hey!

DAVEY. And Belle's brother.

WOMEN. Damn right! *Etc.*

DAVEY. Anyway, I been thinking about joining the Army. There's too many kids in our family, and I won't lie to you — I'm ascared of the mines. I sure would like a chance to see the world, and make thirteen dollars a month for doing nothing, but Mr. Casey here says the Filipinos are people just like us and the government's over there trying to take their country away from 'em. I wouldn't want nothing do do with that. I can't decide, so I'd like for you people to tell me what's right.

Mutters of resentment at this new moral burden.

BELLE. I don't want you to go, but I'll tell you one thing. Casey's crazy when he says the Filipinos are just like us — why they're nothing but ignorant savages!

Whites agree, except Casey.

MONTANA. So go ahead and kill 'em, just like you done the Indians.

HARRY. Hell, we're only killing the bad ones — the good ones, we're going to bring 'em the blessings of democracy!

CASEY. Just like we brought to the Cubans and the Porto Ricans — and now they got martial law in those countries, and the U.S. Army will arrest any worker who goes out on strike. And I'll tell you something else: the Army's five times bigger now than when the war started — and it ain't

going to be long before we're seeing them right here!
General disbelief.

TOMÁS. I don't think you should go — but for a different reason than Casey. I'm against it because if the United States takes over the Philippines, los Filipinos will be coming here to take over our jobs.

HARRY. Cheap labor! You can't organize 'em!

MONTANA. That's what you used to say about the Mexicans.

TOMÁS. But Asians are different!

MONTANA. Oh, I see!

TOMÁS. I worked with the Chinese on the railroad, and I know them. You can't organize Asians!

HARRY. Keep 'em out!

MARIA. Tomás! ¿Cómo puedes decir eso?

TOMÁS. ¡Tú no conoces los Chinos!

CASEY. The people of the world fighting each other for scraps, while the capitalist feasts on the wealth of the earth. All the workers in the world have only got one enemy — and that is the only enemy we ought to fight!

MONTANA. That's the truth.

MARIA. Eso es, hombre.

SLADE. Maybe Casey thinks we shouldn't mine copper.

CASEY. For the imperialists? Maybe I don't!

SLADE. Let's get this straight, now. If we win the strike, we shouldn't go back to work.

CASEY. If the mines and the mills and the factories stopped, it would not be long before this god-damn war stopped!

MARIA. Casey! You're going too far. We shouldn't take back the jobs we've been fighting for? We're poor people — we might like to solve all the world's problems, but we have to draw a line.

CASEY. But where?

BELLE. I'll tell you where — around our own! We been fighting for our rights and we mean to have 'em. I read where this war means a lot more jobs for people here. If that's what it means, it's okay by me.

SLADE. *Returning to chair.* It does — it means markets. And who's going to get fat? The American worker!

> *Harry, miner, Sarah, Belle all tell their neighbors*
> *this is true. Tomás and Maria wonder.*

HARRY. Hell, we ought to be thanking our soldiers — it's clear they're fighting for us.

CASEY. It's the Filipinos that are fighting for you!

BELLE. Casey is crazy!

MONTANA. Casey's right!

> *Everybody turns on Montana.*

SLADE. I call the question. Does the boy go to war for jobs? All in favor.

> *Harry, Slade, miner, Sarah shout 'Yeah!'*
> *Maria, Tomás, Belle vote yes reluctantly.*

Opposed?

CASEY, MONTANA. No!

SLADE. So long, son!

DAVEY. It's a wonderful thing you folks done for me!

HARRY. Keep your head down, Davey!

> *Belle embraces Davey, weeping.*

SLADE. Harry, boy — I got to talk to you for a minute.

HARRY. I don't know, Charlie — is it important?

SLADE. You bet.

HARRY. Belle, I'll see you at home.

TOMÁS. *To Casey.* You just blew a chance to be president.

> *Exeunt all but Maria and Casey.*
> *Montana gives Casey a sad pat as she leaves.*

MARIA. There's another line to be drawn — between what we have to do here and now, and what we want to change in the long run.

CASEY. That's what they tell me — but they don't notice that the long run starts here and now.

MARIA. Tell me this — how will we change anything, if we starve to death first? Piénsalo, hombre. *Exits.*

CASEY. *Sings, 'The Big Picture.'*
Why can't people see the Whole Picture?
We live in the Dark Ages.
Believing in little pictures,
Little fragments, all distorted,
The little pictures of Terror and Destruction.
Who said ignorance is bliss?
Ignorance is the worst tyrant of all.
Spoken. We live in the Dark Ages.
On Monday, we refuse to be victims,
And stand up to the powerful men who own everything.
On Tuesday, we forget who we are.
And praise the great men who steal everything.

75

Sings.
>   Entranced like fools by great men and their hocus-pocus
>   We believe that folks like us, far away, who also fight
>   Are devils.

Spoken. Why can't people see the big picture?
Sings.
>   But who can blame people?
>   Powerful men, who manipulate despair,
>   Control the press, the schools and our imaginations.
>   Little pictures are for sale instead of information.
>   And if you don't have much, it's hard to take
>   exception
>   With men who own it all and plainly threaten,

Spoken. 'You've got everything to lose!'
Sings.
>   Of course we've got the power to overhaul the
>   system.
>   But men who own the military, courts, police and
>   then some
>   Always have a point.
>   And you, Casey, my boy, were a fool.
>   You sprang the trap to press a point,
>   And frightened people whose courage was great.
>   But who can blame me?
>   I can see the Big Picture!
>   And a New Age, a Just and a Beautiful Age
>   Will be brought about by the whole working class.
>   It's so close, and I became impatient.

>   *First deputy enters, gun drawn.*

DEPUTY. Evening, comrade.

>   *Second deputy enters other side.*

You're under arrest.

CASEY. Again?

>   *First deputy handcuffs Casey; second takes his gun.*

What for?

76

DEPUTY. How 'bout destruction of company property —
blowing up the shaft house?

CASEY. You boys got me all wrong. I don't believe in de-
stroying property — I believe in expropriating it.

DEPUTY. How 'bout fornication — with that Mexican
woman?

Casey swings both hands and hits deputy.
They beat him; he falls.

You all right, comrade?

Casey moans.

Kicks Casey several times, hard. Drags him to his feet. You
ain't going to make any more speeches.

Exeunt, Deputies dragging Casey off.

III.5

Montana's, the next morning.
Harry enters, drunk, in work clothes, with gun.

HARRY.
Sings.

Home, home on the range... Is jumping from the frying pan into the... ' *Stumbles, drops gun.*

BELLE. *Offstage.* Harry?

HARRY. Oh, shit.

Belle enters.

BELLE. It's five AM! Where the hell have you been?

HARRY. I been out — on union business. *Puts gun in belt.*

BELLE. Where are you going?

HARRY. You blind? I'm going to work.

BELLE. What are you talking about?

HARRY. Seems to me, you're the one's doing all the talking. I told you I'm going to work. Now move.

BELLE. Not until you tell me what the hell is going on!

HARRY. Nothing special — we decided to call off the strike, that's all.

BELLE. Who is 'we'?

HARRY. Oh, me — and a lot of the other boys, and good old Charlie Slade. 'Strike's adjourned!' And it wasn't a damn minute too soon, neither. You want to know something, Miss Know-It-All? The company's fixing to bring federal troops up in here! That's right — Charlie told me. They told him. They said have us back to work by the end of the week or else it's all over.

BELLE. Why didn't he tell everybody at the meeting?

HARRY. It's them damn hot-headed Mexicans. They'd want to fight the whole U.S. Army, get us all killed. This way, we give them their choice. They can come on back to work with the rest of us, or they can wait till the soldiers get here and round 'em all up, put 'em on a train and send 'em back to Mexico.

BELLE. In other words, you're selling them out.

HARRY. I'm taking care of myself! They can take care of theirselves too. 'Solidarity' — it's a beautiful word; but it ain't going to stand up against the United States Army. So I'm just going to live my life the best I can and take care of my own. Now get out of my way, I'm going to work.

BELLE. You are going to do no such thing.

HARRY. Look here, woman. Don't you EVER tell me what to do and what not to do! *Tries to push past her.*

BELLE. I will when you need telling! *Pushes him.*

They fight, hard. Belle knocks him down. Picks him up.

Get up to bed, Harry — you're drunk.

HARRY. Okay, Belle. *Hits her suddenly and knocks her down.*

Belle? I didn't hurt you, did I, honey? I wouldn't hurt you. *Lifts her.* You're the only reason I'm doing any of this. Christ — why do they wait till we're all wore out and then spring this on us!

BELLE. What about Montana? What about the bar?

HARRY. What about 'em? You want to know something? We don't get nothing. Not now, not the rest of our lives! Nothing. *Exits.*

BELLE. I wish I was dead!

Montana enters.

MONTANA. What's going on down here? *Looks Belle over.* I don't like to say I told you so, so I won't say nothing.

Belle cries.

Shouldn't no one buy a house in fair weather. Cheer up, honey — I got a premonition things about to change. Can't be they're going to get worse, so it must be they're going to get better. Can't you see it? Place all lit up, warm, full of customers — glasses clinking, mirrors shining — and you'll be my singing AND dancing star now.

BELLE. Montana —

Maria enters.

MARIA. The gringos are going back to work.

MONTANA. So that's what she's crying about.

MARIA. She should be. Her husband's in the front of the pack.

BELLE. Charlie told them if they didn't go back to work the company's going to send federal troops in.

MARIA. So you're leaving us to face the soldiers? *She looks at the banner:* 'United We Stand.'

MONTANA. I won't ask what happened to 'Amnesty for Montana.' You drawed your line now.

BELLE. Me!

MONTANA. Sometimes it don't matter what you done. It just matter what your color done.

Maria rips down the banner.

Tomás enters, carrying his rifle.

TOMÁS. It's all over.

MARIA. Tomás, you were right.

TOMÁS. The Mexicanos all took out after the gabachos. Get the women together to stop them from killing each other.

Gunshots offstage. Harry enters.

HARRY. *Calls.* Belle! *Sees women.* Look out here — I got to get my rifle.

TOMÁS. I'm going to kill you.

HARRY. Wait! There's nigger soldiers out there!

More gunshots offstage.

Washington Jefferson enters. He has them covered.

JEFFERSON. And in here. Drop the gun, Pancho.

HARRY. They were waiting for us when we got to the mine.

TOMÁS. You asked for this, pinche vendido.

81

JEFFERSON. Keep the hands up! *To Montana.* Who the hell are you?

All look at them.

MONTANA. A damn fool. And you ain't making me any friends.

JEFFERSON. Okay, relax. Strike's over, folks. U.S. Army going to open up this mine. They got a great big bull pen built up the road, and you all going to sit there until you ready to sign that old yellow dog contract: 'I hereby renounce and forever forswear membership in any labor organization,' then you can go back to work.

MONTANA. You got one of them on you now? 'Cause we got a man here just begging to sign it.

HARRY. No, I ain't! I come back for my rifle.

TOMÁS. You wanted to fight? After you destroyed this whole town? That's funny! *Attacks Harry.*

JEFFERSON. *Stops him.* What's wrong with you people?

MARIA. This man just sold us out.

BELLE. And for nothing. Charlie Slade set you up.

HARRY. Yeah, and he was set up too. He was as surprised as I was — now he'd dead. It was a trap, see, to catch us off guard. Anybody could have fallen for it.

TOMÁS. We passed up our chance to sell you out, remember?

JEFFERSON. White boy tried to save his own ass, huh? Well, the joke's on him. You think you white, you going to come out all right. Far as the man concerned, it don't make no difference. Who is Ed Casey?

They stare at him.

MARIA. Un gringo.

TOMÁS. Ed Casey? He's the man that gave the death blow to this strike, because he cares more about the damn Filipinos than he cares about people right here.

JEFFERSON. I'm worried about the Filipinos, too. But Ed Casey ain't worried about nothing.

They stare at him.

82

Train stopped on up the track a few miles. We supposed to circle the town on foot and sneak up on y'all. Come to cross the railroad bridge, full moon. There was a white man hung from the trestle.

HARRY. Oh God!

They look at him.

They was just going to get him out of town.

JEFFERSON. Strung his ass up just like a nigger, with a big sign across his chest: 'Here Died Ed Casey and the Miners' Union.'

TOMÁS. *To Harry.* Who did it?

HARRY. I don't know.

MONTANA. The long arm of the Amalgamated Copper Company.

HARRY. Belle?

She turns away.

JEFFERSON. Why you want to be so hard on him? Man couldn't hold us down all by himself: he need whitey here, just like he need me. I joined the Army to liberate black folks in Cuba. Know where I'm bound for after I put you in jail? San Francisco — catch a boat for the Philippines.

MONTANA. And kill colored folks that's trying to liberate themselves.

JEFFERSON. No. I got to miss that boat. See, the man go around to each one of us, promising, 'I'll save your people if you help me put down these here. And we do it. And he is the only one that gets saved. That's what your friend there was trying to tell you: too bad y'all didn't listen. Look like the union died sure enough.

MARIA. *Crossing and picking up the crumpled banner.* No. *She hands one end to Belle, and they fold it.* Take us where we're going. *She puts the banner over her arm, in the formal manner of carrying a flag.* It'll be very bad if we don't get there right away.

HARRY. We all going together?

83

TOMÁS. We ain't got no choice.

All but Jefferson freeze.

JEFFERSON. That's right. When the time come, you don't get to pick who's on your side — history decide that for you. You just got to understand history.

Bow.

Exeunt.

San Francisco Mime Troupe

presents

San Fran Scandals

of `73

a
vaudeville
exposé

CHARACTERS

STELLA BARNES. *Vaudeville Song and Dance Woman*
FRANK BURNS. *Her partner*
MRS. SNEATH. *An Agent*
CHERISE FARQUHAR. *Executive Secretary to*
HAROLD P. SMELLYBUCKS. *Millionaire Patron of the Arts*
CARLOTTA SNOTTA. *World's Greatest Soprano*

Note: This (the third and final) version first performed September, 1973. The proposal for a San Francisco Performing Arts Center was advanced for years by the long-time chairman of the city's Art Commission, and heir to the Crown-Zellerbach paper fortune, Harold Zellerbach. Although defeated overwhelmingly at the polls, the center was finally built — with revenue-sharing funds and large private contributions — in 1979.

San Fran Scandals

Frank & Stella's Home.
Stella enters, sets card, 'Barnes and Burns,'
takes a bow.

STELLA.

Thank you. Thank you. But before we go any further I'd
like to introduce the members of the band. Barry, I'd like
you to meet David. David, this is Andrea. Teddy, meet...
Band members shake hands.
Folks, they are a great band, really terrific. Why, last week
they played for two hours and still stumped the panel on
'What's My Line?'...Hit it, boys! *Sings 'Stella's Song.'*
   When she was sweet sixteen, she left her home town
   Packed a little suitcase and caught a Greyhound
   Drove into the station with a twenty dollar bill
   Checked into a room at the Starlet Hotel.
   She pounded the pavement, she got the runaround.
   Agents and producers all turning her down.
   Her future looked grim, her career would have to wait,
   So she spent a few years slinging hash on a plate.
Spoken in time to steps. Five, six, seven, eight — slinging
hash upon a plate. *Sings.*
   Dear Momma, things are going swell.
   Here's a check for two-fifty, hope it finds you well.
   But Momma didn't know that she was down and out
   She was starting to learn what life is all about.

With pathos.
Now it's ten years later, and there's nowhere else to go

Pause.

 Cause she's the star of stage, screen and radio
 And all her success didn't go to her head
 She plans to stop living the day she drops dead.
Oh, thank you. You're so kind. Thank you. And my
partner would like to thank you too, but he's still trying
to fight his way out of the dressing room. Now, I won't say
the dressing rooms in this joint are small, but the rats walk
around hunchback. *Dancing like a hunchback rat.* But this
time I was smart. I changed in the trunk. And, believe you
me, that is a tricky proposition. *Does a fancy step.* And
speaking of tricky propositions, isn't it great the way
President Nixon took crime off the streets and put it in the
White House? You know the motto of the Republican
Party used to be 'Four More Years,' today it's 'Five to
Life.' Ah, but I shouldn't be making all these jokes about
the President; why, he had to go into the hospital for brain
surgery. Really. To remove all his hemmorrhoids. No, I
was just pulling your leg, or anything else I could find;
President Nixon never had hemorrhoids and never will.
You know why? Cause he's a perfect asshole.*

 But enough of these jokes, folks. I'm not out here to
make you cry. My partner will do that. I'm out here to
cheer you up, so you can cheer him up. And believe you me
that is another tricky proposition. *Dance step.* And now,
ladies and gentlemen, I want to introduce you to the man
you've all been waiting for, a little guy with a heart so big
you can hear it from the balcony — a man that's been in
show business so long that every time he opens the refrig-
erator door and the light goes on he does ten minutes: my
partner, Mr. Frank Burns!
   Frank enters, with bags.
FRANK. I got the groceries.

Note: These 'openers' are included to give a sense of style; in practice, the butt
of this opening corn was changed from time to time and place to place.

STELLA. Isn't he just great, folks…Mr. Frank Burns!

FRANK. At it again, huh, Stella?

STELLA. Frankie, Frankie; we're on!

FRANK. Sure, we're on.

STELLA. Atta boy, Frank.

FRANK. We're on welfare, banana brain!

STELLA. Frank!

FRANK. Stella! You are fifty-eight years old. I'm sixty-two. This scroungy dump is our apartment. Nixon is president, and there is no more vaudeville.

STELLA. Frank! You're killing the act!

FRANK. Jesus Christ. Snap out of it, Stella. There's nobody out there. Now tell me, what year is it?

STELLA. 1974.

FRANK. That's right — we have been unemployed for twenty-seven years. Now what happened to the Fox Theater?

STELLA. Office building.

FRANK. What happened to the Orpheum Theater?

STELLA. Parking lot.

FRANK. And what happened to the Golden Gate?

STELLA. Skin house.

FRANK. So what does that make us?

STELLA. Has-beens.

FRANK. Right. Has-beens.

STELLA. Whatever you say, Frank. Well, did you find a job today?

FRANK. Yeah, I found a job — but I didn't take it.

STELLA. You didn't take it? What was it?

FRANK. Practice dummy in a Kung Fu parlor.

STELLA. Well, never mind. It's my turn tomorrow. And, Frank, I've got a feeling our luck's about to change.

FRANK. Sure. Sure.

STELLA. Would ya do the number with me, Frank?

FRANK. No.

STELLA. For old time's sake.

FRANK. Forget old times.

STELLA. Oh, Frankie, I know nobody's out there — but for Baby Taptoes?

FRANK. Well, all right — but I ain't doing no encores.

They do a number — first a soft shoe,
then some banter, like:

STELLA. Frank, you know what I was reading in Reader's Digest?

FRANK. No, what were you reading?

STELLA. I was reading that Wonder Bread is ten times as absorbent as toilet paper.

FRANK. That's terrible. Somebody ought to report them.

STELLA. No, it's okay, because toilet paper is ten times as nutritious as Wonder Bread.

A little yuk, then:

And now, the one you've all been waiting for, that Tiny Titan of Terpsichore — Baby Taptoes. *She opens the trunk to reveal…only a tiny costume.* She's gone, Frank!

FRANK. Of course, she's gone — she's been gone for twenty-eight years!

STELLA. Baby Taptoes, where are you?

FRANK. A poor little orphan child, abandoned on our doorstep —

STELLA. The only baby I ever had!

FRANK. Remember how she used to sing before she could talk even?

STELLA. And when she was still crawling around, she used to try on my tap shoes? Only five years old, and already she knew six steps!

FRANK. Yeah, when YOU LOST HER!

STELLA. Whattya mean I lost her? Who wanted to save the train fare by shipping her in the trunk?

FRANK. Well, who was the genius that gave the stationmaster the wrong address?

STELLA. Baby Taptoes! Please come home. Oh — Your

mama's old, she needs you —

FRANK. Stella, take it easy — she can't hear you.

STELLA. Fly back to your little nest! Forgive me wherever you are!

FRANK. STELLA! Get a grip on yourself!

STELLA. *Suddenly calmer than he is.* Hey, Frank — take it easy.

FRANK. Now, just be thankful we still got our home.
Knock, knock, knock.
Must be termites — nobody ever visits us here.
STELLA. It's the agency. The booking agency, Frank. They're coming to boo...
FRANK. Will you knock it off...
STELLA. This morning in my horoscope it said something big in your future. Frank, you look great — go open the door.
Strikes pose as Frank opens door.
Sneath enters.
SNEATH. Is this 3417½ Schubert, Apartment B?
FRANK. B for basement.
SNEATH. Are your names Mr. and Mrs. Frank Burns?
FRANK. Yes.
STELLA. Stella Barnes and Frank Burns. *Sings.*
We're Barnes & Burns.
FRANK. *Sings.*
We're Burns & Barnes.
STELLA & FRANK. *Sing.*
We always aim to please ya
But if we can't do that you bet
We're surely gonna tease ya.
SNEATH. *Aside.* More casualties along the great highway of progress. *To them.* I am Mr. Sneath of the agency.
STELLA. The agency! Charmed, I'm sure.
FRANK. Ahem, and which agency do you represent?
SNEATH. The Federal Redevelopment Agency. I have come to inform you that this building is about to be razed.
STELLA. Frank, they're finally going to do something about this low ceiling!
SNEATH. I presume you people are aware that this property forms a portion of the site of the future San Francisco Cultural Artistic Complex?
FRANK & STELLA. The WHAT?
SNEATH. The majestic temple to the performing arts which by

93

the year 1984 will occupy this entire city block.

STELLA. A theater! All we have to do is stay right here, and before we know it we'll be right back center stage!

SNEATH. Mrs. Burns —

STELLA. Ms. Barnes. I'm BARNES and that's BURNS, we're Barnes and Burns...

FRANK & STELLA. Burns and Barnes...

They start dancing. Sneath flips out, then screams.

SNEATH. Stoppit! Haven't you read the eviction notices our office has been mailing out for the last 90 days?

FRANK. Eviction notices!

STELLA. Did they come in pink envelopes?

SNEATH. Salmon.

STELLA. Oh, yeah, we got 'em. But I threw 'em out.

FRANK. You threw 'em out!

STELLA. I had to — we were using 'em for toilet paper.

FRANK. Omigod — look, mister, you can't kick us out: see, we ain't had sufficient warning.

SNEATH. What I see, Mr. Barnes-Burns, is that your structure is unsound, your wiring inadequate, and your plumbing is clogged. And since this is the ninetieth day of your ninety-day warning, the bulldozers are now at your door.

Noise.

FRANK. But we've lived here for thirty-five years.

STELLA. Wait a minute — who's in charge of this Cultural Cornflakes?

SNEATH. The Cultural Artistic Complex Committee is headed by Mr. Harold P. Smellybucks, the toilet paper tycoon.

STELLA. Would he go for this? *Demonstrates a step.*

SNEATH. I'm sorry — the Cultural Artistic Complex is a home for the Opera, the Symphony, and the Ballet. *Exits.*

FRANK & STELLA. Hey, you can't do that.

SNEATH. *Re-enters.* Out by five, riff-raff. *Exits.*

STELLA. They can't do this to us.

FRANK. We'll fight it every inch of the way!

STELLA. We're not leaving!

Noise – louder. Set shakes.
FRANK. Say, let's go pay this guy Smellybucks a visit.
STELLA. Yeah, let's go give him a piece of your mind.
Pick up trunk, exeunt.

2.

*Crown Smellybucks office, high atop a downtown
San Francisco highrise. Farquhar enters, sets
sign, 'Crown Smellybucks,' crowned with roll of
toilet paper. Phone rings.*

FARQUHAR.

Good morning, Crown Smellybucks. No, I'm sorry — Mr.
Smellybucks is in conference, Mayor Mafioto. May I
take the message. 'Meet you at the massage parlor in a half
an hour.' Yes, I've got it, sir. Well, arrivaderci to you, too,
sir. And now for today's mail. *Opens letters.*
*Smellybucks enters,
singing to 'Pilgrim's Chorus' from Tannhäuser.*
SMELLYBUCKS. Ich vill ein Culturepalace gebilden soonen.
Miss Farquhar — do I turn you on?
FARQUHAR. Well, in a certain way, sir — I've always found
you grotesque —
Smellybucks gnashes his teeth.
I mean commanding! In spite of your build —
Smellybucks gnashes.
And elegant — even though you're not young.
Smellybucks gnashes.
And then you're so FAMOUS!
SMELLYBUCKS. I am?
FARQUHAR. Everybody knows your name. It's in every
public —
SMELLYBUCKS. Every public toilet? Don't be ashamed, Miss

Farquhar — I'm not. I'm PROUD. Without that little
cylinder sitting there, the San Francisco Ballet would be
dancing on street corners. I know the low jokes they make
about me — but my Cultural Complex will wipe them all
out.

FARQUHAR. I hope so, sir. But, judging by today's mail —

SMELLYBUCKS. Go on — read it.

FARQUHAR. *Shuffling letters.* And I quote. 'Monstrosity.'
'Gigantic ripoff.' 'Taxpayer's nightmare.' 'Screw you,
Smellybucks.'

SMELLYBUCKS. Is there anything else?

FARQUHAR. Well, there is one letter, sir, I hoped you would
listen to.

SMELLYBUCKS. Go on, read it.

FARQUHAR. 'Dear Mr. Smellybucks: Me and my six kids have been living in the same house on Grove Street for the past ten years, ever since my husband Albert, a wonderful man, passed away. Now you tell us we have to leave. All I got to say is, what about me and Ronny, Donny, Lonnie, Bonnie, Connie, and Sleepy? We got no place to go. Please help us out. Yours ever so trustingly, Mabel Jones.' *Sniffles.*

SMELLYBUCKS. The way they nip at my heels. Little people, who want to stand between me and my dream. Look out there, Miss Farquhar. *Motions out window.* What do you see?

FARQUHAR. Glass, concrete, asphalt, steel and smog.

SMELLYBUCKS. The NEW San Francisco. Was it built by little people? Pah! They fought it all the way. And where did that get them? Why, this morning alone we evicted 400 families. Yes, a few great men made San Francisco what it is today. But there is one thing lacking.

FARQUHAR. There's no people.

SMELLYBUCKS. People, schmeople. There's no CULTURE. But my Cultural Complex will change all that. The plans have just arrived from the architect. Feast your eyes on this. *Unveils picture of monstrous building.*

FARQUHAR. Arghhh! I mean aah! It's a dream come true, isn't it, sir?

SMELLYBUCKS. MY dream — and the queen of my dreams is coming to share it with me. Miss Farquhar, I'm expecting a very special visitor.

FARQUHAR. Not John Erlichman?

SMELLYBUCKS. Not today. No, I'm expecting a lady, the greatest living woman artist.

FARQUHAR. You can't mean —

SMELLYBUCKS. I do. Carlotta Snotta.

FARQUHAR. The world's greatest soprano! But she refuses to sing in San Francisco, she says the Opera House is too cramped. She won't sing anyplace smaller than the Coliseum.

SMELLYBUCKS. In Rome?

FARQUHAR. No, Oakland.

SMELLYBUCKS. She will sing here — at the opening of my Cultural Complex.

FARQUHAR. Oh, sir! It's a masterstroke. The public adores her!

SMELLYBUCKS. Yes. She's got the kind of...je ne sais quoi... that really appeals to the little people, and keeps them quiet. She'll be here any minute with her manager, to sign the contract. Let me know the minute she arrives. I'll be in my office drawing up the contract.... And, Miss Farquhar, in the future, try to make your appearance a little more artistic. For a girl Friday, you always look like Monday morning. *Exits.*

FARQUHAR. It's not easy being the perfect secretary. *Sings, 'Farquhar's Song.'*

I type, I file, I take dictation.
Code, collate, open doors,
PBX, do tabulations —
Yet, I long for something more.
   I smile, keep knees crossed, wear foundations,
   Scent, smooth, suntan, sauna, spray,
   Meet, mix, match, take planned vacations —
   Yet, I want to run away.
      Music continues as she speaks.
I, Cherise Farquhar, delivered as a foundling child to the Katherine Gibbs Secretarial School. Why, I could take shorthand before I could write. In fact, I still can't write very well. And now, here I am, personal secretary to Mr. Harold P. Smellybucks.... And yet, deep inside me, is someone I hardly even know...a little stranger...*Begins to tap dance as she sings.*
I feel inside me, strange pulsations,

Can't keep my feet still on the floor.
What are these lovely new sensations,
And yet I've done all this before.
Swept away, she takes a fall. Oh, no! *Scrambles up.* This
must be the influence of my mysterious past, about which
I know nothing!

3.

Stella enters, bumps into Farquhar.

STELLA.
Is this Mr. Smellybucks' office?

FARQUHAR. *Taking her for Carlotta Snotta.* Why, yes it is...
oh, Madam, can I get you someth...ah...how do you like
our view?

STELLA. Your view?
Farquhar indicates the window and the view of the city.
Stella does a take and gets sick. Excuse me, honey, but
heights make me nauseous. *Totters.*
Farquhar grabs her.

FARQUHAR. Oh, I'm sorry.

STELLA. Oh, that's nothing. Frank's scared of elevators. He's
walking up...forty-three flights! *Laughs.*
Farquhar is staring at her.
Hey, is my face on crooked or something? You're staring at
me awful funny.

FARQUHAR. I'm terribly sorry. It's just that I have this feeling
I've seen you someplace before.
They do a take, are whammied.
Farquhar recovers first.
Oh, well, it must be because you're so famous.

STELLA. Famous?! You mean you remember me?

FARQUHAR. Why, Madam, you're unforgettable.
     Stella is ecstatic.
I'd better get Mr. Smellybucks. He's inside, drawing up the contract.

STELLA. Contract! *Grabs Farquhar.* What contract?

FARQUHAR. The contract for your appearance at the opening of the Cultural Complex. I'm sure he'll be as thrilled as I am. *Exits.*

STELLA. Contract — opening — Frank!
     Frank enters, dragging trunk.

FRANK. *Mimics her.* 'Frank!' Whattaya leave me with the trunk for?

STELLA. Frank — he knows us! He wants us! He's going to give us a contract!

FRANK. Not again. Stella, we're here on important business.

STELLA. What did I tell you? I told you, I had this feeling.

FRANK. Please, Stell. I know the air's very thin up here.

STELLA. It's true, Frank. He's in there. He's drawing up the contr...

FRANK. Shh! Now calm down and let me do the talking.

STELLA. Frank, I think I'm going to faint. *Faints.*
     Smellybucks sings offstage, enters with Farquhar.

SMELLYBUCKS. *Aside.* I must make her love me the instant she sees me.

FARQUHAR. She's right over — EEK! Ms. Snotta!

SMELLYBUCKS. Bellissima, ravississimma, intoxicantissima signora — what happened?

FRANK. Oh, it's nothing. She's tired, so she's taking a little coma. Anyway, I'm the one that does the talking. Are you Mr. Smellybucks?

SMELLYBUCKS. Harold P. at your service.

FRANK. My name is Burns. Frank Burns of Burns & Barnes.

FARQUHAR. Burns & Barnes?

FRANK. Some people say Barnes & Burns, but some people will say anything.

Farquhar and Frank do a take.

SMELLYBUCKS. Miss Farquhar — water!

Farquhar exits.

Mr. Burns, I must tell you that this is the woman I love.

FRANK. *Indignant.* What?

SMELLYBUCKS. It's true — I love Carlotta with all my heart.

FRANK. Carlotta?

SMELLYBUCKS. Carlotta Snotta, the world's greatest living
soprano.

Farquhar enters.

FARQUHAR. I got it, I got the water. *Spills it on Smellybucks.*

SMELLYBUCKS. Miss Farquhar!

She dries him off.

Out!

Farquhar exits.

Ah! How I have longed to hear those golden notes emerge
from your alabaster throat.

STELLA. Oh — uh... You're too kind.

SMELLYBUCKS. I knew your beauty would equal your talent.

STELLA. Well, it's swell meeting you too!

SMELLYBUCKS. To think that for half a lifetime I have been deprived of both, by the chintziness of the average tax-payer.

FRANK. What are you talking about?

SMELLYBUCKS. Simply: I have tried to build a theater equal to her art, but... Miss Farquhar!

Farquhar enters.

FARQUHAR. The little people wouldn't let him.

STELLA. Oh, that's terrible.

SMELLYBUCKS. For decades, I, and men like me, have struggled with that insoluble city problem... Farquie?

FARQUHAR. How do you build something for rich people, and get poor people to pay for it?

FRANK. Hmmmm... Oh, yeah, now that's a tricky proposition!

FRANK & STELLA. Hey, hey, hey, hey. *They do a fancy step.*

SMELLYBUCKS. How charming — how fresh — how new! But now we have a solution. Farquie?

FARQUHAR. Revenue sharing. The federal government takes their tax money, and hands it over...

SMELLYBUCKS. No strings attached!

FARQUHAR. To the city government.

SMELLYBUCKS. In other words, to me. This time we have the land, the plans are drawn, all we have to do is clear away the riff-raff.

FRANK. Riff raff?

SMELLYBUCKS. Mr. Burns, we are all set to spend 100 million dollars of the taxpayers' money, and the damn fools don't know a thing about it.

FRANK. I protest.

SMELLYBUCKS. Oh, there are protestors, of course, but with your name on the contract we will smother their cries.

STELLA. My name?

SMELLYBUCKS. Put in any figure you like.

STELLA. I will.

SMELLYBUCKS. When you step on that stage on opening night, you will make me the happiest man in the free world. *Kisses Stella's hand.* I must depart before I say too much. Addio, bellississima signora.

STELLA. Bela Lugosi to you to.

Smellybucks and Farquhar exeunt.

Frank, that guy loves me!

FRANK. Yeah, he loves you, alright!

STELLA. He knows talent! He's gonna give us our big break. Didja see him kiss my hand?

FRANK. I saw. I SAW!

STELLA. Now, Frank. Don't be jealous. It's not just me. It's both of us. Just like old times. You remember, Barnes & Burns?

FRANK. Stella! That guy thinks you are somebody else.

STELLA. Oh, no, Frank! He remembers me. Like old times, Frank. The Roxy, the Foxy. He was outta his mind....

FRANK. He thinks you are Carlotta Snotta.

STELLA. Carloada what?

FRANK. Carlotta Snotta, the famous opera singer.

STELLA. Frank, you really kill me. You really do. I am finally getting some recognition for my great talent after all these years, this billionaire is kissing my hand, and you...you're telling me that he thinks that...I'm CARLOTTA SNOTTA? THE FAMOUS OPERA SINGER? He doesn't remember us? He's not gonna sign the contract? Oh, Frank. We're HAS-BEENS. We were born has-beens. Gee, and he was such a nice guy too.

FRANK. Nice guy? That's the guy who's kicking us out of our home! It's guys like him that killed vaudeville. Stella, he wants to make us live in Brisbane.

STELLA. BRISBANE! Frank, Frank, ya know what I'm gonna do to that guy?

FRANK. No, what, Stella?

STELLA. Well, first I'm gonna lean on him. You know, LEAN on him.

FRANK. Make him get hot round the collar.

STELLA. Then I'm gonna tear off his arms. Then I'm gonna tear off his legs. Then I'm gonna chop off his head and throw it in his face. After that, I'm gonna kill him.

FRANK. STELLA! We don't wanna kill him. We wanna use him!

STELLA. Right. We don't wanna kill him, we wanna use him. Then we'll kill him. Now, how do we use him?

FRANK. Well, he thinks that you are Carlotta Snotta, right?

STELLA. Right.

FRANK. So we'll make him a tricky proposition.

FRANK & STELLA. Hey, hey, hey, hey. *They do a fancy step.*

FRANK. Listen —
                    They whisper. Farquhar enters.

FARQUHAR. Mr. Smellybucks sent me to inquire if you are through perusing the contract.

STELLA. We didn't bruise it, we were very careful with it.

FRANK. Would you shut up and let me do the talking? Now look here, Ms. Carfare.

FARQUHAR. Farquhar.

FRANK. Farquhar. Miss Snotta, her and me, we've got a few fine points we'd like to wrinkle out.

FARQUHAR. Very good, sir. I'll just tell Mr....
                    Elevator noise.

STELLA. It's the elevator.

FRANK. The elevator.

FARQUHAR. The elevator. Who could that be?

FRANK. Whoever it is, would you please get rid of them?

FARQUHAR. I'll do my best, sir. How very strange. We weren't expecting anyone else.
              Carlotta Snotta enters in sunglasses, fur, etc.

CARLOTTA. Is thees the office of meester Smallpox?

FARQUHAR. Smellybucks. Yes it is. And whom shall I say is intruding?

CARLOTTA. I'm Carlotta Snotta.

FRANK, STELLA, FARQUHAR. Carlotta Snotta!

CARLOTTA. Quite a thrill, isn't it? I always get a big reaction when I say it. Ecco. Carlotta Snotta!

FRANK, STELLA, FARQUHAR. Carlotta Snotta!

FARQUHAR. Oh, no!

CARLOTTA. Of course you don't recognize me. I must travel in disguise. Otherwise I have little pipple crowding all over me! Ugh! They touch me, they ask me things, they want me to sing. That's disgusting. I don't sing for nothing. When I hit the high 'C' the glass she break. Ecco. *Sings.*
                    Set shakes.

FARQUHAR. Not here, madam. We're pressurized.

CARLOTTA. Where is Mr. Smellybox?

FARQUHAR. He's right inside. I'll get...

FRANK. *Grabs Farquhar.* He's not here.

CARLOTTA. Ees not here?

STELLA. He's in the trunk.

CARLOTTA. The tronk!

FRANK. Yea — that is, he's not there yet, but...

STELLA. He'll meet you there!

CARLOTTA. Why?

FRANK. Why?

STELLA. Why?

FARQUHAR. Um — because of all the little pipple!

CARLOTTA. Pipple.

STELLA. They heard you were coming. The building's crawling with them. They're coming up the fire escapes. They all
want your autograph.

CARLOTTA. The tronk, the tronk. *Gets inside.* You tell 'im to hurry, eh. I am, how you say, closet-phobic.

FRANK. Pretend you're somebody else.

They shut her in trunk.

Lock that box, shut that nut up.

FARQUHAR. Yeah, and write if you find work.

STELLA. Yeah, write if you find work.

FARQUHAR. I have the feeling she's going to go far.

FRANK. In the trunk, huh?

FARQUHAR. I always wanted to hear her sing a solo. So low you couldn't hear it. And now Mr. Smellybucks thinks that you're Carlotta Snotta, right? But Carlotta Snotta's really locked inside this trunk. And when Mr. Smellybucks finds out, he's gonna blow his stack. He'll probably call the police…

FRANK & STELLA. Police!

FRANK. Now look here, Miss Farquhar, we didn't mean nothing by it.

STELLA. It was just a little joke.

FRANK. Don't call the police.

FARQUHAR. I'm not gonna call the police.

FRANK. You're not?

FARQUHAR. Heavens, no.

STELLA. Why not?

FARQUHAR. I hate Mr. Smellybucks. And it's not just his insulting remarks — 'Miss Farquhar, that dress makes you look like a mailbox; let's play post office.' But it's not just that. Look what he's done to our city. He's kicked thousands of people out of their homes.

FRANK & STELLA. We know.

FARQUHAR. A guy like that who owns property he doesn't even know about. Forests in Canada, lumber mills in Chile, packaging plants in Oakland.

FRANK. And now he wants to build this artsy-fartsy complex that no one can buy tickets to.

FARQUHAR. Yeah. $9.50 a seat.

FRANK. $9.50? That's two hamburgers!

STELLA. Remember the Orpheum, Frank?

FRANK. Anybody could come.

STELLA. A full house every night.

FRANK. Eight shows a day, 365 days a year.

STELLA. Boy, did we pull 'em in at the box office — yeah, and what did we get out of it?

FRANK. Nothing, that's what!

STELLA. Frank, it's the same old routine! After forty-five years in show business.

FARQUHAR. First you do the show, then you get the business.

STELLA. It's time to do something about it.

FARQUHAR. I don't know who you folks are, but I get a funny feeling we can work together. Got the contract?

FRANK. Right here.

FARQUHAR. Let's change it.

ALL. Hey, hey, hey, hey. *All pore over contract, laughing.*

SMELLYBUCKS. *Offstage.* Carlotta, Carlotta. Ready or notta, here I come.

FARQUHAR. He's coming. Are you ready?

FRANK. All right, Stella. Now, who are you?

STELLA. I'ma Carlotta Snotta.

Smellybucks enters.

SMELLYBUCKS. Goddess, command me. Are you satisfied with the contract?

STELLA. Contract. You call this a contract? This is toilet paper. *Blows nose in it.* Spumoni, Mozzarella, Andy Granatelli.

SMELLYBUCKS. Please, Carlotta, I'll change anything you say.

STELLA. And this place.

FRANK & FARQUHAR. This place?

STELLA. You want Carlotta to sing in a place like this? I don't sing in a place like this. I'm gonna show you what I do in a place like this. *She starts to squat.*

SMELLYBUCKS. Please, Carlotta. *Aside.* She's so hot-blooded.

STELLA. Manischewitz. Karmen Ghia!

SMELLYBUCKS. Add anything — but don't say you won't sing!

STELLA. Okay.

FRANK. Miss Farquhar will now read the revived contract.

FARQUHAR. Ahem. 'Mr. Harold P. Smellybucks hereby agrees to resign from the Art Commission and to turn the commission over to the artists and people of the neighborhoods.'

SMELLYBUCKS. People of the neighborhoods? What about the Opera, the Symphony, the Ballet?

FRANK. What about singers, and comedians?

STELLA. And the old soft shoe.

SMELLYBUCKS. I don't believe what I see.

STELLA. To dance is to love, Smelly.

SMELLYBUCKS. Can we get on with it?

FARQUHAR. 'Furthermore, Mr. Smellybucks agrees to destroy no more houses, and to build new housing, inside the city, for all the poor people he has dislocated.'

SMELLYBUCKS. House the riff-raff. You people strike at the very heart of redevelopment. You drive a very hard bargain.

FRANK. Well, she is the world's greatest opera singer.

STELLA. *Sings.* AAAGGGH.

FRANK. *Croaking along with Stella, but only to stop her.* Aaaa…not another note until he pays.

SMELLYBUCKS. Can we get to the part about your performance at the complex?

FARQUHAR. 'Finally, and last but not least, if the rich people of this city desire a complex for their artsy activities, let them build it with their own smelly bucks. They will not touch a penny of the public taxes, which will go to the people who really need it.' That is all. Sign here, sir.

FRANK. Sign here, sir.

STELLA. Sign here, sir.

SMELLYBUCKS. This is ludicrous. You leave me nothing. You give me the shaft.

FRANK. You better sign it, Harold.

SMELLYBUCKS. This death warrant? Why should I? No destruction, no complex. No complex, no opening night. No opening night, no Carlotta!

FRANK. If you don't sign, we're gonna sue you.

SMELLYBUCKS. You sue me? What for?

FRANK. We're gonna sue you…for…for…for…

FARQUHAR. Chafing!

STELLA. Chafing!

SMELLYBUCKS. Chafing?

FRANK. We are gonna say that Carlotta Snotta here was chafed by your toilet paper.

SMELLYBUCKS. Carlotta!

STELLA. I have such sensitive skin.

FRANK. So we're gonna sue you.

STELLA. And then we're gonna kill you. And then we're gonna throw you in jail.

FRANK. Twenty-five years for manchafing. Ms. Snotta, tell the court exactly how it felt.

STELLA. It was just like ground glass.

SMELLYBUCKS. Heartless beauty. Farquie, Farquie, what

should I do? They're planning to wipe me out with my own
tissue.

FARQUHAR. Tissue? Tissue? I don't even know you.

FRANK. That's farkin' him, Tellie.

SMELLYBUCKS. All right — I'll sign. Is there anything else?

STELLA. Yes, take my make-up case over to the opera house.
Points to trunk.

SMELLYBUCKS. The opera house?

FRANK. We're doing the mugging of Vigoro. Vigoro, vigoro,
vigoro.

SMELLYBUCKS. It's very heavy.

FRANK, STELLA, FARQUHAR. So are we.

> *Smellybucks exits with trunk.*

112

FRANK. *Runs to phone.* Hello, police emergency. If you come to the lobby of the Smellybucks Building in the next ten minutes, you can catch the Pacific Heights Trunk Murderer. He's the one with the trunk.

STELLA. He's about to dispose of his latest victim.

Frank breathes into phone.

FARQUHAR. Have a nice day.

FRANK. Hey, we did it, Farquie. You were great.

FARQUHAR. Say, were you two folks really in show business?

STELLA. Frank, let's do the number for Farquie.

FRANK. Sure, Stella.

STELLA. And now, direct to you from San Francisco...

FRANK. We're Burns and Barnes.

STELLA. We're Barnes and Burns. We always aim to please you.

FRANK. But if we can't do that you bet...

FRANK & STELLA. We're really gonna tease you.

FRANK. And now the one you've all been waiting for...

STELLA. That Tiny Titan of Terpsichore...

FRANK. The Biggest Little Star in Heaven...

FRANK & STELLA. Baaaby Taptoes!!! *They start to weep.*

Farquhar comes forward, does tap step.

FRANK. No, no, it can't be Baby Taptoes. Cause Baby Taptoes had kinky orange hair.

FARQUHAR. *Takes off wig, revealing curly orange hair.* Mama Barnes, Daddy Burns... *Takes off dress, revealing grown-up version of costume in trunk.* It's me!

FRANK & STELLA. Baby Taptoes!

ALL. *Dance and sing.*

> We feel inside us strange vibrations
> They've always used us 'cause we're poor
> Tell them to keep their mausoleum
> Don't let them screw us anymore,
> Don't let them screw us anymore!

THE SAN FRANCISCO MIME TROUPE IN:

THE DRAGON LADY'S REVENGE

COMING SOON!

115

CHARACTERS

HAROLD SAUNDERS. *The Private*
CLYDE DILLSWORTH JUNKER III. *The Lieutenant*
A MYSTERIOUS PRIEST
TRAN DOG. *The Servant*
CLYDE DILLSWORTH JUNKER II. *The U.S. Ambassador*
GENERAL RONG Q. *The Head of State*
BLOSSOM. *The B-girl*
A MYSTERIOUS FAKIR
THE DRAGON LADY
REVEREND TIM DROOLEY. *The Counter-Insurgency Agent*
A MYSTERIOUS FENCING STUDENT
A MYSTERIOUS FENCING INSTRUCTOR
A MYSTERIOUS NUN
MR. BIG

PLACE: *Long Pinh, capital of Cochin, a small nation in Southeast Asia*
TIME: *Around the middle of the 20th Century*

Note: Opened August, 1971, in Washington Square Park, San Francisco. The play was inspired by an August, 1971, *Ramparts* article (we saw it in galleys) by Banning Garrett and Frank Browning, which broke the story of the CIA's involvement in the Indochina drug trade. Its closing run — when it won an Obie — was in New York in December-January 1972-1973, during Nixon's 'Christmas Bombing' of Vietnam.

116

The Dragon Lady's Revenge

PROLOGUE

A street in Long Pinh.
Harold enters, sick.

HAROLD.

Where is he?

Clyde enters, discovers Harold.

CLYDE. My God — Saunders! Is it really you? What's happened, man? You look awful!

HAROLD. This is no place for you, lieutenant. You'd better go back to the base and leave me alone.

CLYDE. Say, is that any way to talk to an old buddy? Look — I know this great little place where we could go for some tea — the atmosphere is really authentic!

HAROLD. Just get out of here, Clyde — I'm meeting someone and I don't want you around.

CLYDE. Knock it off, Harry. Listen, if you're worried about being AWOL, forget it — I have influence.

HAROLD. Open your eyes, Clyde. Look at me — what I need right now is a fix! I'm here to cop and my pusher is late. Man, if he sees you, he's not going to come near me!

CLYDE. I won't leave you like this, Harry — you've got to come back with me and see a doctor!

HAROLD. I can't go back — the drug's only part of the reason. The rest you don't even have a glimmer of. But it's big, Clyde — really big, and I know too much about it to go back with you.

117

CLYDE. What are you talking about?

HAROLD. Oh, shit — I'm going to be sick — bring me that garbage can. *Points.*

> *Clyde moves, Harold dashes off.*

CLYDE. What garb — there are no garbage cans in Asia! Harry! *Follows Harold off.*

> *Drooley enters, disguised as priest, through trap door*
> *marked 'Sewer.' Harold enters.*

HAROLD. You got the stuff?

DROOLEY. I got it. *Pulls out heroin addict's outfit; his crucifix is the* syringe.

> *They prepare the fix. Clyde enters. Harold kneels;*
> *Drooley hastily makes sign of the cross.*

In Nomine Patrium Filii Spiritu Sanctum.

CLYDE. How moving. Harry's taken the first step toward rehabilitation. Amen.

> *Harold shoots up. Drooley exits.*
> *Harold staggers to his feet, smiling.*

To know God is indeed...

> *Harold falls.*

Harry!

HAROLD. O.D.... double-cross — got to stop... White Monkey... c... l... aaa... *Dies.*

CLYDE. Harold — murdered! What did he say? O... D — odd! Got to stop — odd white monkey! Harry, I swear, over your dead body, that I shall not rest until I have avenged your death! *Carries body off.*

INTRODUCTION

TRAN DOG

In a time not so distant from our own, the western empire set out to conquer the east. The armies of the west were the most powerful the world had ever seen. Some easterners, who thought the invaders would surely win, joined them. Others waited for the outcome. Many more were determined to resist. Each year, the west sent more soldiers. Each year, the eastern soil put forth more defenders. But the west was proud, and determined to conquer — until its army was stricken by a terrible sickness. The affliction spread through the ranks, until the army was greatly weakened; then crossed the sea and struck the empire in its very heart — its children. No one could understand this misfortune.

Kind ladies, honorable gentlemen, comrades — the San Francisco Mime Troupe proudly presents THE DRAGON LADY'S REVENGE.

I. 1

The American Embassy.
Tran Dog enters, starts dusting.
Ambassador enters.

AMBASSADOR.

Tran Dog! They told me about you. How long have you worked here at the Embassy?

TRAN DOG. Since French leave.

AMBASSADOR. And before that?

TRAN DOG. I work for Japanese.

AMBASSADOR. And in all that time you've never been tempted to run away and join the nationalists — the revolutionaries?

TRAN DOG. I take my bowl to man who serve rice. *Holds hand out.*

AMBASSADOR. Ah, Tran Dog — if more people were like you, we'd have an easier time keeping the peace in this world. *Gives him money.* Here — buy yourself something to smoke. I'm expecting your President, General Rong Q. What kind of man is he? What do the people say about him?

TRAN DOG. Very smart man. Very big pockets.

AMBASSADOR. Big pockets, eh? Just what they told me at the briefing.

Bell rings.

Show him in.

Rong Q enters.

TRAN DOG. General Rong Q, Mister C. Dillsworth Junker — new American Ambassador. *Bows out.*

AMBASSADOR. Good afternoon. Do you speak English?

RONG Q. I received my B.A. degree from Michigan State University.

AMBASSADOR. The Spartans!

They shake hands.

RONG Q. I need many things. The situation is not good. We want to fight — we are very warlike — but we cannot fight with old weapons. I plan to march to the North. For this I need planes. I need helicopters. I need bombs. I think the time may be ripe for — Secret Weapon X-90!

AMBASSADOR. General! I am not here to talk about classified weapons. My President dispatched me to deal with your health crisis.

RONG Q. I do not understand.

AMBASSADOR. ADDICTIVE DRUGS.

RONG Q. No.

AMBASSADOR. ILLICIT NARCOTICS.

RONG Q. No.

AMBASSADOR. SMACK?

RONG Q. I understand.

AMBASSADOR. Once, it lurked in the ghettos — okay — but now it's reaching our suburbs, and the American people and my government will not stand for it!

RONG Q. Very serious problem. I think maybe it is a Communist plot, calling for extreme solution — X-90!

AMBASSADOR. Out of the question! If the drug trade is a Communist plot, a surprising number of your people are growing rich on it. Look, Rong Q — Long Pinh is well known as the capital of the drug trade. Beginning immediately, you must clean up the city. I see you are angry.

RONG Q. Have I not always been a faithful friend of the U.S.? In or out of office have I not always served your government? Have I not fought the Communists for 20 years? And now I am rewarded with insults and distrust!

AMBASSADOR. Oh, come now, General —

RONG Q. Perhaps I have made a mistake. Perhaps, if you no longer have confidence in me, I could reach an agreement with the other side.

AMBASSADOR. Perhaps. But there are many ambitious generals in your country, and my President has asked me to advise him as to which one merits our confidence. If you get behind our cleanup campaign, I am prepared to offer you the presidency here for life.

RONG Q. How can this be arranged?

AMBASSADOR. Through free and democratic elections.

RONG Q. To sterilize Long Pinh will not be easy, Ambassador.

AMBASSADOR. Who is the number one drug supplier in the area?

RONG Q. Some say it is a female, known as the Dragon Lady, who operates out of a nightclub called the White Monkey Bar — very popular with your G.I.s.

AMBASSADOR. Start there. I want her closed down.

RONG Q. The Dragon Lady is a very powerful woman.

AMBASSADOR. But, fortunately, only a woman.

RONG Q. Not exactly. Behind her, there is said to be a mysterious Mr. Big.

AMBASSADOR. You deal with the Dragon Lady. The American government will take care of this Mr. Big.

RONG Q. It would be easier if the American government supplied Secret Weapon X-90.

AMBASSADOR. The American government has learned to be cautious about military solutions to political problems.

Exeunt.

123

I. 2

The White Monkey Bar.
Clyde enters, searching.

CLYDE.
I've been to the White Monkey Laundry, the White Monkey Fortune Cookie Factory, the White Monkey Teahouse...
Blossom enters behind him.
...and now I've come to the White Monkey Bar.
Music. Blossom dances.
This must be the place. *To Blossom.* Uh...do you speak... English?

BLOSSOM. Yes, sir. The Americans have been in my country ever since I was born. So — this is your first visit to the White Monkey Bar?

CLYDE. Yes, well — I usually go to the officer's club.

BLOSSOM. Ah! You are officer? You must have a lot of men in your command.

CLYDE. Oh, not too many — 150 or so.

BLOSSOM. *Taking notes.* That's a lot!

CLYDE. You really think so?

BLOSSOM. Um hm. I bet you got a lot of big guns, too.

CLYDE. Yeah — a lotta big men, a lotta big guns.

BLOSSOM. What kind of big guns you got?

CLYDE. We got 60s, 90s...

BLOSSOM. APCs?

CLYDE. Twenty-four APCs.

BLOSSOM. Half tracks?

CLYDE. Twelve half tracks, each mounted with a 24 millimeter recoilless cannon on each turret, and what not.

BLOSSOM. What's a whatnot?

CLYDE. Forget that... I'm looking for a priest.

BLOSSOM. At the White Monkey Bar?

CLYDE. That's just it! Do you know one?

BLOSSOM. Anything can be arranged, sir.

CLYDE. Say — what kind of a place is this?

BLOSSOM. I think you are beginning to understand.

CLYDE. Poor Harold!

BLOSSOM. Harold?

CLYDE. Don't deny it, baby — you know who he was.

BLOSSOM. Not I, sir — I cannot tell one American from another.

CLYDE. Drop the act. Harold was murdered by enemy agents who hooked him in the first place — Commie agents who stoop so low they disguise themselves as priests!

*Drooley enters, disguised as a fakir,
with suitcase marked 'Air America.'*

DROOLEY. *Aside.* The kid!

CLYDE. The more I think about it the more it disgusts me! This place is probably a Commie front! Sometimes it seems like everyone in this darn country's the enemy.

BLOSSOM. Why don't you go home, then?

CLYDE. *Sees Drooley.* All right — *pulls gun* — don't move. *To Blossom.* Who's that?

BLOSSOM. He's what you might call a faker.

DROOLEY. FAKIR.

BLOSSOM. He does business here.

CLYDE. What's in the suitcase, fakir?

DROOLEY. Nothing in the suitcase — just some junk, that's all.
Case falls open, brick-shaped packages fall out.

CLYDE. Well, get your junk together and get out of here.

BLOSSOM. Put that gun away, you crazy.

CLYDE. I could never shoot a woman anyway. *Puts gun away.*
I've got to find out where that priest is!
Hands emerge from back curtain, take suitcase from Drooley.

BLOSSOM. It's not the priest you should be after.

CLYDE. I've got to get to the bottom of this.

BLOSSOM. Why not get to the top?

CLYDE. So you do know something.

BLOSSOM. Just as a stream is to the sea, so is that priest to Mr. Big.

CLYDE. Mr. Big?

DROOLEY. *Eavesdropping.* Mr. Big!

CLYDE. Back off, fakir. As the sea is to the river, so is the stream to Mr. Bigfoot —

BLOSSOM. No.

CLYDE. Who is this Mr. Big?

DROOLEY. Mr. Big again.

CLYDE. Is the priest connected to Mr. Big?

Blossom nods.

DROOLEY. That's one question too many! *Attacks Clyde.*

CLYDE. Wait! *To Blossom.* Looks like there's going to be a little rough stuff here, Miss. You'd better step aside.

Drooley knocks Clyde off stage; he climbs back.

All right.

Drooley sprays Clyde with mace; he falls.

My eyes!

DROOLEY. Technology!

BLOSSOM. Could you hold this for a minute? *Hands Drooley her nail file, wastes him with two karate chops, kicks him off stage.*

CLYDE. Wow! Where did you learn to fight like that?

BLOSSOM. In the mountains. *Helps him up.*

Gong. Dragon Lady enters.

DRAGON LADY. What is all this commotion?

CLYDE. Who's THAT?

BLOSSOM. That's the Dragon Lady. Everything is in order now, madam. *Exits on signal from Dragon Lady.*

DRAGON LADY. Tell me, lieutenant — is this rowdiness the customary behavior of officers visiting the native quarter?

CLYDE. I... well... you ought to know, toots!

DRAGON LADY. My, how ardent. You'd better run along now back to your barracks, before it's too late.

CLYDE. But I have to speak with you. It's very important!

DRAGON LADY. I'm sure it is, lieutenant, but it's well past bedtime, so if you'll excuse me...

CLYDE. Harold Saunders! Did you know him?

DRAGON LADY. Saunders? *Smiles.*

CLYDE. I think he was murdered!

DRAGON LADY. You are no doubt correct, but if you are smart, you'll take my advice and leave the dead alone.

CLYDE. It's my duty to find his murderer.

DRAGON LADY. Very noble, my dear Boy Scout. You know you're not dealing anymore with the U.S. Army, lieutenant.

CLYDE. You can't frighten me.

DRAGON LADY. As you wish. Tell me — does not my humble establishment interest you? Every evil known you can find here, my friend: gambling, whiskey, special massage...or is it something else that might interest? There is a plant grown in the highlands of my country, known as the flower of Nepenthe. As you may know, this is the house specialty.

CLYDE. I know all about that filthy poison you people are killing our soldiers with. Poor Harold! Get away from me, murderess!

DRAGON LADY. Did you know, lieutenant, that this poison was spread throughout Asia, in the last century, by the British and French colonialists? Very profitable, and very soothing to the population. Do you know who Nepenthe was, lieutenant?

CLYDE. Why — she was the goddess of sleep and dreams!

DRAGON LADY. I see you are not a high school dropout, lieutenant. *Sings, 'Song of the Nepenthe Flower.'*

    Look on the ruin and wrack
    Of generations that have gone before:
    First the Japanese, then the French — oo la la la —
    And now, they tell me, the American war.
    Is it the fool going where the angel fears to tread?
    Take the sleep of Nepenthe — give in
    Dream the dream of Nepenthe,
    And float forever to the sea.
            Clyde is captivated; they dance.
    So take a look at the river
    As it floats from Long Pinh to the sea —
    Can you swim against that strong current?

CLYDE. Yes!

DRAGON LADY. *Sings.*

    Never! Think it over, I'm sure you'll agree.
    So take the sleep of Nepenthe — give in.
    Dream the dream of Nepenthe
    And float forever to the sea.

They sink to the floor. Dragon Lady caresses Clyde's arm,
then plunges a giant syringe into his vein.

DRAGON LADY. Blossom!

Blossom enters.

I think we have a new client.

BLOSSOM. Yes...

Rong Q staggers through curtain, drunk and disheveled.

RONG Q. Dragon Lady! I have something to discuss with you.

DRAGON LADY. *To Clyde.* Welcome to the White Monkey Bar, lieutenant. *Goes to Rong Q.*
> *Rong Q and Dragon Lady argue.*

CLYDE. *Rising languorously.* All RIGHT! *Gets sick.* I don't feel so well — can you take me home?

BLOSSOM. Where is your home?

CLYDE. The American Embassy.
> *Gong.*

DRAGON LADY. How can you betray me like this?

RONG Q. Oh, shut up, you sniveling bitch!
> *Rong Q and Dragon Lady exeunt.*

CLYDE. Can you get me home all right?

BLOSSOM. You're in safe hands, my friend.
> *Exeunt. Blossom carries Clyde off (if possible).*

II.1

> *The Embassy, the next morning.*
> *Tran Dog enters, dusting.*
> *Clyde enters, distracted, runs into Tran Dog.*

CLYDE.

Gon on — get out of here.
> *Tran Dog gives him a long look before departing.*

Just as the river is to the priest — that's not it. Just as —
> *Ambassador enters.*

AMBASSADOR. Good morning, son!

CLYDE. Good morning, dad.

AMBASSADOR. It's swell to be together again. Although the servants tell me you were a bit under the weather when you came in last night.

CLYDE. A bit.

AMBASSADOR. A lot of temptations out here for an American boy. I remember Singapore when I was your age. We'd just licked the Japs, and the entire Pacific basin lay spread out before us like some vast green orchard of soft, ripe fruit... I remember the scent of jasmine, and a Eurasian beauty so eager to please... but it's best to take these things in moderation, Clyde. You don't want to let Asia get under your skin.

CLYDE. Dad — why are we here?

AMBASSADOR. You ask questions now, like all the restless inquiring young folk in your generation. And that's why I'm here, to answer your questions. What was the question?

CLYDE. Why are we here?

AMBASSADOR. Petroleum is part of the answer, but only part. Basically, we are here because we desperately want to get out.

CLYDE. I don't get it.

AMBASSADOR. The President has promised that he will wind down this ugly and unpopular war. And we have implemented orderly withdrawals of our troops to neighboring countries. But, realistically, we cannot get out of this war until we can trust the people here to go on with it.

CLYDE. That's the part I don't understand.

AMBASSADOR. It's our only hope, Clyde. In the words of Harry S Truman: 'The American system can only survive if it becomes the world system.' And that's how it is, my boy: a struggle to the death between capitalism — what we call democracy — and communism. And we can't just let this struggle work itself out in the marketplace, because communism has an unfair advantage.

CLYDE. What's that?

AMBASSADOR. People like it. That's why the most peace-loving nation in the world has been at war with the world since the World War. But what's got you worried, son?

CLYDE. It's — sometimes I get the feeling the people here just don't like us.

AMBASSADOR. That's a feeling you'll learn to live with, Clyde

— I did. And it isn't that bad: I'm going to show you that the average Asian basically appreciates what you can do for him. *Calls.* Tran Dog! *To Clyde.* I'm going to introduce you to a real character.

Tran Dog enters.

TRAN DOG. You call, sir?

AMBASSADOR. Tran Dog, my son the lieutenant here feels that your people don't like the American soldiers. What do you say to that, Tran Dog?

TRAN DOG. My people very ignorant — very poor people. Sometimes they think American have too many dollar. *Puts hand out.*

Ambassador gives Clyde money to give to Tran Dog.
Tran Dog smiles.

You see? Everybody rich, everybody like everybody. Hee, hee, hee.

AMBASSADOR. *Joined by Clyde.* Ha, ha, ha.

TRAN DOG. You likee Long Pinh, lieutenant?

CLYDE. Er — yes, it's a very interesting city.

TRAN DOG. Got gambling, whiskey, girls — very good for American. But one thing very bad — Nepenthe flower. You stay away!

AMBASSADOR. Very good advice, Tran Dog, though I doubt my boy — what's the matter, son?

CLYDE. It's dope, dad! Dope! That's what's on my mind!

AMBASSADOR. Oh, no!

CLYDE. No, not me, dad — not me! It killed one of my men — he died in my arms. Harold!

AMBASSADOR. That's tough, son.

CLYDE. And it's everywhere. They say fifteen percent of our soldiers are hooked — that's hundreds of thousands of addicts created by this war! And it's all a huge sea of corruption. Harold didn't just die — he was murdered! Murdered because he knew too much!

AMBASSADOR. Did he tell you what he knew?

CLYDE. He gave me one clue. I followed it out and discovered there's a Dragon Lady in it — and a Mr. Big.

TRAN DOG. Mr. Big!

Ambassador and Clyde stare at Tran Dog.

Everybody hear of him — nobody know him!

AMBASSADOR. Clyde — you haven't asked your dad why he's here.

CLYDE. Why are you here, dad?

AMBASSADOR. On special assignment — to clean up the dope trade.

CLYDE. Dad — that's great!

AMBASSADOR. And, I don't mind telling you, I've made considerable headway.

TRAN DOG. HEAD way? *Exits.*

CLYDE. Boy, we really need you here, dad — and I think I can help!

AMBASSADOR. You can help all right, son — by staying as far away from this thing as possible.

CLYDE. But, dad —

AMBASSADOR. No buts. If these drug people found out who you were, they might try to harm you to get back at me.

Doorbell.

I'm expecting one of the key people in our strategy.

Drooley enters disguised as a Jesus Freak.

DROOLEY. Bom Maharishi! Haftarah shanti shanti Jesus loves you!

AMBASSADOR. This is the Reverend Tim Drooley. Tim — my son, Lieutenant C. Dillsworth Junker III.

DROOLEY. *Aside.* The kid!

CLYDE. How do you do?

DROOLEY. What's happening? *Checks Clyde's arm.* Yeah! My friends call me Spike.

AMBASSADOR. You might not know it to look at him, but Spike here is a medically trained missionary, and he's setting up our methadone program for us. We feel that he's

the right kind of person to deal with our drug-dependent
G.I.s.

DROOLEY. God plus methadone equals Hope.

CLYDE. What's methadone, Spike?

DROOLEY. Methadone is the only sure cure for junk. It's the
cool drug — you don't get sick, you don't get high: you just
stay on it.

CLYDE. How come?

DROOLEY. Because it's ten times as addictive — yeah — and
the government gives it away for free. And it's a clean drug,
lieutenant; it comes in a nice clean white Dixie cup. Like
which would you choose, lieutenant — this? *Shows cup.* Or
this? *Shows needle.* I didn't mean to freak you out,
lieutenant.

CLYDE. *Aside.* My god — the priest!

AMBASSADOR. That's a very effective demonstration, Spike.
We'll remember your technique when we set up our NEXT
methadone center.

DROOLEY. Isn't one enough?

AMBASSADOR. I intend to clean up this city. I'm going to start
at the bottom and go straight to the top!

DROOLEY. You're going to take on Mr. Big?

AMBASSADOR. Just how much of this drug traffic does Mr. Big
really control?

DROOLEY. He's the Superstar — the big cheese — and he eats
too much meat. You're a heavy cat yourself, Ambassador —
a very heavy cat. A crusader against junk... but this is the
twentieth century, and crusaders have got to be careful.
Dig it?

AMBASSADOR. Thanks for the advice, Tim. I'll try to get some
press boys down there to do a story for the American
public.

DROOLEY. That's where it's at, Ambassador. Now I got to
split. I got to see a man. Later, lieutenant, and remember,
'The meek shall inherit the earth' — but 'Woe to him who

seeketh after knowledge, for he shall know no peace.' Peace!
Gives 'V' sign, exits.

AMBASSADOR. I'd have thought you'd get a positive hit off of
Tim.

CLYDE. *To audience.* Oh, my God — what'll I do? I can't tell
him.

AMBASSADOR. What's the matter, son?

CLYDE. I've — got to see a man, too. Goodbye, dad. Be
careful! *Exits.*

        Tran Dog enters with glass on tray.

TRAN DOG. Very big hurry.

AMBASSADOR. *Drinks.* I wonder what's gotten into that boy.

        Exeunt.

II.2

*A street in Long Pinh. Drooley enters through sewer,
disguised as a fencing student. Clyde enters running.
Drooley, as if by accident, stops him with foil.*

DROOLEY.

Excusez-moi.

CLYDE. Did you see a goofy-looking guy in a platinum wig and
dark glasses come by here?

DROOLEY. *With French accent.* Goofy-looking...? I do not
believe so. Why are you looking for him?

CLYDE. I saw him kill my best friend, Harold Saunders!

DROOLEY. So...you are an eyewitness to a murder.

CLYDE. The only one, too.

DROOLEY. How interesting to meet you all alone on this
deserted street.

CLYDE. Doesn't it just make you want to puke? The hypocrisy
in this world!

DROOLEY. You don't know the half of it.

CLYDE. He was disguised as a priest. He had the hat, he had the robe, he had the rosary; he even had the cruci — *Recognizes Drooley's hypo-cross.*

BOTH. FIX!

Clyde gets it in the vein.

DROOLEY. Okay, dough-boy — who else have you told about this priest?

CLYDE. Blossom...

DROOLEY. *Dumps Clyde down sewer, sings 'CIA Song.'*
   I am the prototype of an agent of intelligence

I graduated Yale, I have mixed with men of affluence
I give guns here, junk there — I inspire confidence
From Michoacan to Katmandu to counterbalance
    insurgence.

CHORUS. *Sung by musicians.*
To counterbalance insurgence!

DROOLEY.
Of the Bay of Pigs the press was moderately critical
With the Gulf of Tonkin, citizens grew skeptical
Thus embarrassed, Washington conceded points political
But the budget's growing yearly

CHORUS.
Yearly, yearly, yearly

DROOLEY.
For my service indispensable.

CHORUS.
His service indispensable.

DROOLEY.
You've heard about the Halls of Montezuma — Shores of
    Tripoli
But blood and guts has been replaced with an updated
    policy:
Infiltration, co-optation.

CHORUS.
Murder!

DROOLEY.
For democracy — after all
What ship of state could stay afloat

CHORUS.
Glug, glug, glug, glug.

DROOLEY.
Without its counter-insurgent agency?

CHORUS.
Its counter-insurgent agency.
                    Drooley exits.

II.3

*A Fencing Salon. Blossom enters disguised as a
fencing master, hangs sign, 'Fencing Salon,' exits.
Rong Q enters, in fencing gear.*

RONG Q.

At last I can tell that second-rate James Bond exactly what I
think of him. I am going to lay it right on the line. 'Tim,
you rotten, hairy, son of a bitch...'
Drooley enters.

DROOLEY. Yes, Q?

RONG Q. Tim!

DROOLEY. Q! New development to discuss with you.

RONG Q. No, new development to discuss with YOU.
Blossom enters as fencing master.

BLOSSOM. Messieurs. La classe commence.
Drooley and Rong Q take positions.
Un, deux, trois, quatre, cinq, six! En garde, messieurs.
Drooley and Rong Q fence; Blossom stands observing.

RONG Q. Now get this. The chicken has decided to fly the
coop.

DROOLEY. WHAT?

RONG Q. The sheep has found greener pastures.

DROOLEY. Have you gone batshit?

RONG Q. The kiwi has found new boots to polish.

DROOLEY. What are you trying to say, Q?

RONG Q. I'm getting out of the trade, pinhead!

DROOLEY. You can't get out.

RONG Q. Oh, yes, I can.

DROOLEY. You need us, Q.

RONG Q. No, I don't — Tim.

DROOLEY. Yes, you do!

RONG Q. *Swinging sword.* No — I — don't!

DROOLEY. You can't get out — you're essential to the operation!

RONG Q. Perhaps — but I no longer NEED an operation. *Puts up sword.* You see, if I get out, the Ambassador has offered me the Presidency for life.

DROOLEY. *Aside.* Oof. It takes us ten years to set up a perfect network, and Washington sends us an amateur who tears it down in one day!

RONG Q. So, if you'll excuse me, I'll go take a shower and work on my election speech.

DROOLEY. Too bad we can't discuss — X-90!

RONG Q. X-90?

BLOSSOM. X-90?

They stare at her.

Ahem — what is this X-90?

RONG Q. Something like H_2O. I am very thirsty. Go and get me a glass of water.

BLOSSOM. Mais, monsieur —

RONG Q. Go!

BLOSSOM. Continuez la classe!

They resume. She exits.

RONG Q. X-90? You can't get it for me.

DROOLEY. Listen, Q. Who set you up in business?

RONG Q. You did, Tim.

DROOLEY. Who stuffed the ballot boxes and got you elected?

RONG Q. You did. And who sent troops swarming all over my country and made a mess out of everything?

DROOLEY. That was the Pentagon, not the CIA!

RONG Q. Bullshit!

DROOLEY. And when those troops are gone, you're going to be all alone, Q.

RONG Q. Alone?

DROOLEY. Surrounded by Commie hordes! They'll be coming at you, Q — from all directions. Their mouths foaming with red saliva —

RONG Q. We've got to stop them!

DROOLEY. And now we CAN stop them — with this miracle weapon. It's new, it's revolutionary, it destroys the enemy without touching the ecology — X-90.

RONG Q. But the Ambassador told me it was out of the question.

Blossom enters.

DROOLEY. Then we must eliminate the Ambassador. *Discovers Blossom.*

BLOSSOM. Your drink, monsieur.

RONG Q. *Drinks, spits.* This — is — water!

BLOSSOM. But you asked for water!

RONG Q. I never drink water. Go and get me a cheeseburger.

BLOSSOM. Continuez! *She exits.*

RONG Q. You...would have me...kill the Ambassador?

DROOLEY. That's right, Rong.

RONG Q. How?

DROOLEY. This is a perfect assignment for the Dragon Lady.

RONG Q. But I've already told her I have to shut her down!

DROOLEY. She has reason to do away with the Ambassador — more reason than she suspects. *Shows Rong Q a photograph. Blossom enters.*

BLOSSOM. No cheeseburger. Golden Arches closed. *Signals them to resume.*

They fence.

DROOLEY. The Ambassador's son was seen last night at the White Monkey Bar. I have gained intelligence from him that a certain Blossom might be wise to our activities.

RONG Q. Blossom!

BLOSSOM. Recommencez, messieurs!

They do.

DROOLEY. I'll take care of the kid. I leave Blossom to your imagination.

RONG Q. But I have no imagination!

DROOLEY. *To Blossom.* Je suis fini.

RONG Q. Et moi aussi.

BLOSSOM. JE suis fini. Les classes sont finis. *She exits, but eavesdrops on what follows.*

RONG Q. Tim, about X-90 — what exactly is it?

DROOLEY. X-90 is a fatal viral disease, developed in our Presidio laboratories, that preys on the chromosomal characteristics of Orientals.

RONG Q. What does this mean?

DROOLEY. A disease that attaches itself only to yellow skin.

RONG Q. Only to yellow skin? It's perfect — you see, all my enemies — all the communists — they all have...yellow skin. *Sees own hand, screams.* Tim! What about me?

DROOLEY. Don't worry, old man. With you, it's only skin deep.

Exeunt.

Blossom enters, removes mask.

BLOSSOM. So. The disease that attaches itself only to yellow skin — is that what they will send in place of bombs? I know they will stop at nothing, but how far that goes still surprises me. Now — how do I stop those dogs from getting a free hand?

Clyde enters in pursuit, drugged.

CLYDE. Fencing... Fencing Salon. *Sees Blossom, pulls gun.* Hold it right there.

BLOSSOM. Lieutenant. What happened? *Sees his arm.* Not again?

CLYDE. Doesn't matter — I know who killed Harold. It was... the Reverend Tim Drooley.

BLOSSOM. Drooley! I have just learned that he is the U.S. counter-insurgency agent who is working with General Rong Q.

CLYDE. That's impossible. That murderer doesn't work for my government. No.

BLOSSOM. They're planning to kill your father.

CLYDE. Dad? But why?

BLOSSOM. Because your father wants to clean up the dope trade — and he is the only obstacle to Secret Weapon X-90.

CLYDE. So the Reverend and the General are really Commie agents...

BLOSSOM. No, they are really anti-Commie agents, and the dope trade holds their mercenary forces together. Junk is the mainline of Tim Drooley's policy. But never mind that now — you've got to hurry! Go warn your father of the plot against his life! And remember — you're in danger! Don't stop for anyone you may meet. Remember your mission.

Both start off in opposite directions.

CLYDE. Blossom — aren't you going to come with me?

BLOSSOM. I have to get back to the White Monkey Bar. I must reach the Dragon Lady before Rong Q does. *Going.*

CLYDE. Blossom?
BLOSSOM. Yes, lieutenant?
CLYDE. Blossom...?
BLOSSOM. Yes, lieutenant?
CLYDE. Gee, Blossom, you're swell!
Exeunt.

II.4

A street.
Drooley enters through sewer, disguised as a nun.
Clyde enters running.

CLYDE.

I've almost completed my mission!

DROOLEY. *Hobbling. Shrieks.* Oh, pain! Distress!
CLYDE. What's this? A nun in distress?
VOICES. *From backstage.* Remember your mission!
CLYDE. I must not stop for anyone I may meet. *Starts off.*
DROOLEY. Oh, agonizing pain!
Clyde hesitates.
VOICES. Remember your mission!
DROOLEY. Pain, pain, pain!
CLYDE. Can I help you?
DROOLEY. Yes. *Jumps into his arms.*
CLYDE. Jesus Christ. You're heavy.
DROOLEY. Oh, soldier! Please don't take our Lord's name — in vein! *Shoots Clyde with hypo-cross, dumps him down sewer. Takes a bow and follows.*

If intermission is desired, this is the place for it.

II.5

The White Monkey Bar.
Dragon Lady enters, upset.

DRAGON LADY.

Blossom! Bring me my tranquilizers!
Blossom enters, hands Dragon Lady money,
which Dragon Lady begins counting.

BLOSSOM. Madame! General Rong Q is about to shut us
down.

DRAGON LADY. I know.

BLOSSOM. We've got to do something!

DRAGON LADY. Here, count this. I find it has a soothing effect.

BLOSSOM. If I were you, I would kill that viper before he
killed me. I happen to know that the General is on his way
here now, to say that he is your friend.

DRAGON LADY. How grotesque!

BLOSSOM. Will you be ready for him?

DRAGON LADY. *Sings.*

> He won't be the first
> I know his two-faced kind
> He won't be the last
> To die before his time.
> > I was born to fight
> > I fought right from the start.
> > Someone crosses me,
> > I tear the fool apart.
> When I was young I trusted a man.
> He left me flat, didn't give a damn.
> Since that day I've had my way.
> Since that day I've made my way — alone!

BOTH.

> There're always those who try

145

To make our lives their own.
They'll get you if they can,
They'll tear you to the bone.
  We've always fed their needs,
  The men who prey on us.
  It's when we've learned their tricks
  That things begin to change.
When you know the moves they make,
Then you know the move to take.

DRAGON LADY.
  I fight — alone!

BLOSSOM.
>   We fight — together!

DRAGON LADY. *Spoken.* Blossom, for one so young, what do
you know?

BLOSSOM. *Sings.*
>   I know what life can be:
>   Simple harmony.
>   We were of the land.
>   We shared our days together.
>   Working in green fields,
>   Mountain tops, morning mists.
>   Then I saw my village burning,
>   Saw my family dying.
>   When we saw the planes returning
>   We all left our homes.
>   Forced into the city,
>   How we fight to stay alive.
>   So I'm here to work for you —
>   Please soldier to survive.

BOTH.
>   There're always those who try
>   To make our lives their own.
>   They'll get you if they can...

DRAGON LADY. *Spoken.* I'll cut him down, I'll win!

BLOSSOM. *Sings.*
>   Killing the General is all very fine.
>   Why not see something bigger this time?
>   If you were fighting for more than YOURSELF
>   How much greater your victory would be —
>   TOGETHER!

DRAGON LADY. *Cuts off music.* Don't preach! I need no one —
and I DON'T like to share. Here. *Hands Blossom money.* Put
this away and bring me my headache box.

>   *Blossom exits with money,*
>   *returns with jeweled box containing hypo.*

BLOSSOM. Pretty strong for a headache, don't you think?
Doorbell chimes.
DRAGON LADY. Go and see if that's my headache coming on now. *Hides needle in hair.*
Blossom ushers in Rong Q.
RONG Q. Surprised to see me, Frou-Frou?
BLOSSOM. The perpetual puppet — I mean President — at the White Monkey Bar!
RONG Q. *Ignores Blossom.* I have good news!
DRAGON LADY. Have they offered you the throne?
BLOSSOM. Perhaps they are going to make him the first Asian Pope.
RONG Q. *Stroking Blossom's neck menacingly.* What a charming young girl — always laughing and joking — what a pity! Dragon Lady, I wish to speak to you — ALONE.
DRAGON LADY. Go and play with your dolls, Blossom.
Blossom exits through beaded curtain, but spies on following.
So, toad — you've returned.
RONG Q. I could not stay away.
DRAGON LADY. You make me sick.
RONG Q. You hate me, don't you? Well, go ahead, hate me — I deserve it. *Grovels.*
DRAGON LADY. This is not a screen test, Q. What do you want?
RONG Q. I want the fire of your breath — the cold caress of your talons — the blinding gleam of your syringe. I want us to kill the Ambassador.
DRAGON LADY. So the worm has turned. Now you want the Ambassador dead. What's in it for you, Q?
RONG Q. A new weapon. X-90, the disease fatal to all Asians.
DRAGON LADY. Have you lost what little mind you had?
RONG Q. No, simply I am no longer Asian.
DRAGON LADY. Oh, come off it!
RONG Q. The agency assured me. With this weapon I can have total victory — as soon as we kill the Ambassador.

DRAGON LADY. What do you mean, WE, white man? *Takes hypo from hairdo.* I'm going to kill you, Q.

RONG Q. But what about my plan?

DRAGON LADY. I prefer mine. Say goodbye to rainbows, ice cream sodas, and the monsoon season you love so well — . *Advances.*

RONG Q. Wouldn't you rather kill — Dillsey?

DRAGON LADY. *Stops dead.* Dillsey?

RONG Q. Yes. DILLSEY.

DRAGON LADY. No! It can't be...

RONG Q. It is. Clyde Dillsworth Junker II — the new American Ambassador!

Gongs crash.

DRAGON LADY. The only man who ever crossed me and lived. At last fate has brought us together...my revenge must be exquisite.

RONG Q. And that young officer you ENCHANTED last evening —

DRAGON LADY. The kid?

RONG Q. His name is Clyde Dillsworth Junker III.

DRAGON LADY. His son! It's perfect. Oh — come to me, my handsome devil. How could I resist the man who provides me with a perfect revenge!

They kiss. She whips him with her feather boa.
He begs for more until his ecstasy is complete.

RONG Q. What are you going to do now, Frou-Frou?

DRAGON LADY. I think we'll invite His Excellency to a special celebration.

RONG Q. A party! I like it — I like it very much, only there is just one more little thing — *Tiptoes to curtain, reaches in suddenly and pulls Blossom out by the wrist.* Blossom knows too much.

Blossom turns to Dragon Lady, who turns away.
Rong Q brandishes needle.

BLOSSOM. *To Dragon Lady.* You're making a bad mistake!

RONG Q. See you at the party, Frou-Frou. *Exits with Blossom.*

Dragon Lady starts to exit.

Gong, cymbals, drums. Mr. Big enters, masked and hooded,
huge, in dazzling Chinese robes.

DRAGON LADY. You! *Falls to knees.* But I wasn't expecting you —

MR. BIG. *Intones.* Listen to me, Dragon Lady. Do not interrupt or question what I have to say. The time has come to close down our operation.

DRAGON LADY. WHAT?

MR. BIG. SILENCE! We seek new markets. Things have grown too complex here. We must leave Long Pinh immediately.

DRAGON LADY. But —

MR. BIG. YOU DARE TO QUESTION MR. BIG?!!!!

DRAGON LADY. So — the White Monkey Bar is to be closed after all. I have been happy here.

MR. BIG. No sentiment, please.

DRAGON LADY. Forgive me, O faceless one. But I beg of you — give me until midnight. I must take care of one last detail.

MR. BIG. Till midnight, then. I SHALL RETURN! *He sweeps off.*

DRAGON LADY. So little time — and so much to be done. My last and greatest soirée at the White Monkey Bar. *Exits.*

III. 1

The Embassy, that night.
Tran Dog enters, dusting.
Ambassador enters, carrying letter.

AMBASSADOR.

Your famous Dragon Lady breathes out more incense than fire. She has just sent me an extremely sweet-scented message. *Reads.* 'When the eagle soars, all the beasts tremble, but the Dragon's heart quivers with love.' Then, she invites me for cocktails. What do you think? *Sniffs letter.*

TRAN DOG. I am reminded of ancient proverb, 'When wind blows very hot, beware of snakes in the grass.'

AMBASSADOR. Snakes in the grass, eh? Number one snake is that idiot, Rong Q. Despite the promise I got from him yesterday, the White Monkey Bar is still doing business. And Drooley — oh, I don't doubt he's competent, but sometimes I wonder if the Agency knows what it's up to.

TRAN DOG. Ambassador, you no get too deep in this White Monkey business. I think you better stay home, maybe?

AMBASSADOR. To stamp out the drug trade, I'm prepared to

151

take a few risks. Here, take my acceptance to the Dragon Lady.

TRAN DOG. She-Dragon magnificent creature. But, very dangerous.

AMBASSADOR. Wait for me there. And if there's any trouble, don't hesitate to use this. *Gives Tran Dog gun.*
        Tran Dog fumbles with this strange object.
Who knows? Perhaps she might even introduce me to Mr. Big. *Exits.*

TRAN DOG. Maybe not even Dragon Lady can do that, Ambassador. *Twirls gun, does quick draw routine, laughs, exits.*

III. 2

A dungeon beneath the White Monkey Bar.
Rong Q throws Blossom on, laughs nastily.
Blossom's hands are in chains.

RONG Q.

So, my little Blossom. This will teach you not to meddle. *Exits.*

BLOSSOM. Where am I?
        Sign appears: 'In the clutches of the CIA.'
        Clyde enters, drugged, moaning.
So, I'm not alone. Hello? Who's there?

CLYDE. I must save... save... father...

BLOSSOM. Oh, no! Lieutenant! It's me, Blossom!

CLYDE. *Tries to grab her.* Blos...som...Baby...

BLOSSOM. No! Did you reach your father? Did you warn him?

CLYDE. Fa-ther. I must warn father...*Passes out.*

BLOSSOM. Oh, no! He's probably on his way to the White Monkey Bar right now. This is ridiculous: me trying to save the American Ambassador? Well — the enemy of my enemy is my ally, for now. Get up!

Clyde gets up, suddenly alert, then collapses on her again.
Okay. We're going to go for a little walk. *Walks Clyde around stage, counting paces.*

CLYDE. The clouds are parting. I can see clearly now.

BLOSSOM. Can you untie this?

Drooley enters in trench coat, knocks Clyde aside.

DROOLEY. Cute couple. They ought to make a movie about you, 'G.I. Junkie Meets Commie B-Girl.'

BLOSSOM. Very amusing. You could show it as a double feature with 'Priest Gets Creased.'

DROOLEY. Jesus loves you, lieutenant. Booster time! *Holds out hypo.*

Clyde hesitates, licking lips.

BLOSSOM. No. don't do it!

CLYDE. Just this once. *Takes needle.*

BLOSSOM. No!

CLYDE. Shut up! *Shoots up.*

DROOLEY. *Holds Blossom, forcing her to watch. Hooks her bound hands to curtain pole.* Now, sonny ready to see daddy?

CLYDE. Da da.

BLOSSOM. Why do you waste so much time doing evil, when you know you're going to lose the war?

DROOLEY. So, you want to talk politics. *He kisses her.* What's your Red Book say about that?

Blossom spits in his face.

Oh, a little spit-fire! Here's a trick I learned at Yale. *Pulls back curtain, revealing torture machine. Turns switch, machine advances on Blossom.* Struggle, sister! *Exits with Clyde.*

Blossom struggles, machine bears down on her.
Tran Dog enters through sewer.

BLOSSOM. You... old man... up here! The switch! Get the switch!

Tran Dog turns it off just in time, releases Blossom.

153

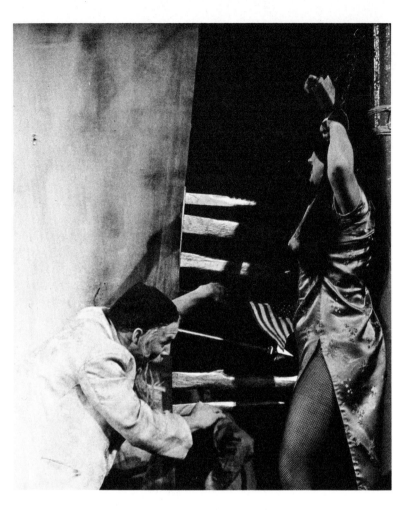

But, who are you?
> *Tran Dog puts finger to lips, hands her a gun.*
> *Both exeunt through sewer.*

III.3

> *The White Monkey Bar. Dragon Lady enters with*
> *goblet on tray, followed by Rong Q, drinking. As he talks,*

she sets tray, produces poison vial, mixes cocktail.

RONG Q.

Oh, Frou-Frou, you look terrific. Think of it — by this time tomorrow, I shall rule Long Pinh supreme and unchallenged. X-90, priceless potion. I wonder how it works? *Reaches for goblet to drink.* Mmmm, what is this?

DRAGON LADY. I wouldn't touch that if I were you. That is a special cocktail for the Ambassador. I think it will intoxicate him — permanently.

RONG Q. What a woman. Don't think, my dear, that I will ever forget the part you played in my rise to power.

DRAGON LADY. Will you continue to adore me, General, after X-90 has attached itself to my yellow skin?

RONG Q. *Shrinks in disgust.* Ugh! But maybe there's a cure.

DRAGON LADY. And, anyway, do you really think Drooley will give it to you?

RONG Q. He promised!

Bell rings. Drooley enters with Clyde.

DROOLEY. Where do you want the kid stashed?

CLYDE. Da da.

DRAGON LADY. The usual place. Now when I give the signal I want him to come out, crawling like a baby.

CLYDE. Da da.

Drooley stashes Clyde.

RONG Q. You are such a character, Tim! Did you bring it, X-90?

DROOLEY. Sure thing, Q. Say, how about getting me a drink first?

RONG Q. Good idea, let's all get drunk. *Exits.*

DROOLEY. Jasmine — JASMINE. *Kissing her.*

DRAGON LADY. Please, Tim — not now.

DROOLEY. You always say that — and I always let you get away with it — why? Because I always put the operation before everything! Well, listen, I got some news for you:

Q's cuckoo! He's a threat to the operation.

Rong Q returns with drink.

RONG Q. I want to see it now, Tim!

DROOLEY. Is this Scotch? *Takes sip.*

RONG Q. No. Japanese.

DROOLEY. Get me a Coke.

Rong Q exits again.

When you finish with the Ambassador, I'm taking care of Q.

DRAGON LADY. It's convenient, but what will you replace him with?

DROOLEY. Ever hear of General Big Dong?

DRAGON LADY. No, but he sounds all right.

DROOLEY. He's trustworthy, levelheaded, ruthless, cunning, corrupt —

DRAGON LADY. Who is he?

DROOLEY. MYSELF! From here on out the Agency takes no chances.

Rong Q, tipsy, enters with Coke.

RONG Q. Tim, they only had it in the can.

Bell rings.

DRAGON LADY. At last — after 25 years!

Ambassador enters in full evening dress.

AMBASSADOR. Permit me to introduce myself. My Excellency, C. Dillsworth Junker.

DRAGON LADY. Life has named me the Dragon Lady.

The Ambassador bows.

I think you know General Q?

AMBASSADOR. Why, yes. We had a long talk only yesterday. But I'm afraid there was a failure of communication. *Takes Coke, as if Rong Q were a waiter.*

RONG Q. Not really — merely a change in situation. *Falls down drunk.* Oh, excuse me.

DRAGON LADY. And of course you know Mr. Drooley.

DROOLEY. Hare rama, Ambassador.

AMBASSADOR. I think we can speak English now, Tim.

DROOLEY. *To Ambassador.* I don't trust these people any farther than you can throw them.

AMBASSADOR. Admirable prudence.

RONG Q. Tim — let me look at it!

DRAGON LADY. Since you gentlemen are already acquainted, why don't you retire to the billiard parlor?

RONG Q. Good idea. Tim — let me see it.

DROOLEY. Don't touch me!

RONG Q. Don't hit me!

Both exit, fighting.

DRAGON LADY. Well, Ambassador. My humble premises blush at the honor you do them.

AMBASSADOR. Yes, it's a magnificent setting.

DRAGON LADY. Why don't you come closer and admire the jewel?

AMBASSADOR. I can see it from here, thanks. It's a dazzling antique. Dragon Lady, I came here to talk to you man to man.

DRAGON LADY. *Offers goblet.* Have a drink then.

DROOLEY. *Offstage.* I said no, Q.

AMBASSADOR. Drooley's in it with you, isn't he? Well, don't expect any protection from him. I want you to close up shop and get out of town.

DRAGON LADY. You know — you amuse me, Ambassador. Why should a man of the world, like yourself, get so upset over a simple thing like my humble product?

AMBASSADOR. I don't expect you to understand. *Sips Coke.* Here in Asia, a human being's just so much garbage. *Tosses can offstage.*

DRAGON LADY. So, you're not a newcomer to the East then, Ambassador?

AMBASSADOR. I spent the best years of my life here.
                    More argument backstage.

DRAGON LADY. You must have known many of our women.

AMBASSADOR. Pearls of the orient without number. There was one in particular — a common bar girl in Singapore. Funny, I couldn't remember her face if my life depended on it, but I'll never forget the smell of — *sniffs* — jasmine...

DRAGON LADY. *Offers drink.* Try my cocktail, Ambassador. It's guaranteed to bring back those old times.
              Ambassador takes goblet, still in reverie.
                  Still more argument backstage.

AMBASSADOR. Look, Dragon Lady. The American government is prepared to make you an offer.

DRAGON LADY. What is it?

AMBASSADOR. A million dollars. To take your business elsewhere — anywhere we don't have an army.

DRAGON LADY. And where might that be, Ambassador?

AMBASSADOR. There must be some place.

DRAGON LADY. A million dollars. I wonder if you know what my business is worth.

AMBASSADOR. That's our offer. You can think about it and let me know. *Tries to hand goblet back.*

DRAGON LADY. Wait. It's not out of the question. I might accept... I accept!

AMBASSADOR. Swell!

DRAGON LADY. On one condition — that we drink to it.

DROOLEY. *Offstage.* I said NO, Q!

RONG Q. *Offstage.* I said YES, Tim!

AMBASSADOR. Oh, did I forget to mention that I never drink alcohol? *Hands back goblet.* But I'll gladly shake on it.
Dragon Lady is agitated.
Why, it's an old custom in...

DRAGON LADY. *Pulls gun.* So you still remember Singapore, eh Dillsey?

AMBASSADOR. Singapore — Dillsey — Jasmine — it's you! How awkward!
Rong Q throws Drooley onstage and jumps on him,
knocking Dragon Lady's gun out of her hand and offstage.

RONG Q. White devil!

DROOLEY. Yellow dwarf!
Rong Q and Drooley fight all over stage. General chase ensues.
Ambassador vanishes. Finally Drooley staggers on,
quaffs goblet, falls off edge of stage and freezes, paralyzed,
as on a cross. Dragon Lady enters, doesn't see him.

DRAGON LADY. Junker's gone! Idiots! Animals! I'll sauté your livers!
Twelve gongs. Mr. Big enters.

MR. BIG. Have you completed your preparations?

DRAGON LADY. Oh, these idiots let the prize slip through my fingers!

MR. BIG. But what have you done to Drooley?

DRAGON LADY. *Sees Drooley for first time.* The cocktail!
Rong Q groans backstage. Dragon Lady opens beaded curtain,
Rong Q falls out dead, a giant hypo stuck in his back.

MR. BIG. Dragon Lady, you never cease to amaze me. The most sordid tasks accomplished with such a flair. You leave me nothing to do — except this. *Pulls gun.*

DRAGON LADY. What?

MR. BIG. You've received your last shipment.

DROOLEY. *With great effort.* No...no...no.

MR. BIG. Farewell, Dragon Lady — and you too, Drooley. You have served me well. But I have no choice — it's the law of the market.

DRAGON LADY. You can't do this!

MR. BIG. You can't stop me. *Takes aim.*

    Blossom enters in black pajamas, with submachine gun.

BLOSSOM. But I can. Reach for the moon, Mr. Big!

MR. BIG. Who are you?

BLOSSOM. A soldier of the People's Liberation Forces. And who are YOU?

MR. BIG. Commander of the capitalist legion. Would you like my card?

BLOSSOM. Very amusing. You stop at nothing! *Pulls Clyde onstage.*

DRAGON LADY. What are you doing?

CLYDE. I know... who you are... you're Mr. Big, the real killer! *Tries to attack him.*

MR. BIG. *Overpowers him without effort.* My God — Clyde! Who did this to you?

DRAGON LADY. 'Clyde'?

BLOSSOM. You did — *Pulls his mask off* — AMBASSADOR!

DRAGON LADY. Dillsey!

CLYDE. Dad!

DROOLEY. No — no — no. *Dies.*

AMBASSADOR. Please, son, I know this looks bad — but don't judge me too quickly.

BLOSSOM. Is the American government behind the dope trade, or is the dope trade behind the American government?

AMBASSADOR. Can you understand me, son?

CLYDE. Go ahead, dad.

AMBASSADOR. The drug trade is exceedingly profitable. Our government, as you know, encourages profit.

CLYDE. But it's criminal!

AMBASSADOR. Can anything that makes billions REALLY be called criminal?

DRAGON LADY. So — your cleanup campaign was just a publicity stunt.

AMBASSADOR. With a solid basis in fact — we are rerouting the traffic to the mass market.

DRAGON LADY. Where?

BLOSSOM. The United States. They found it works better on their people than on ours.

AMBASSADOR. Picture them, Clyde: hundreds of unemployed, discontented young people, many of them racially disgruntled — we've found an efficient, pharmacological way of keeping them happy.

CLYDE. I'M not happy.

AMBASSADOR. I'm sorry, son. That's what happens when a powerful weapon falls into the wrong hands.

Blossom keeps Ambassador back with gun.

DRAGON LADY. Are these the wrong hands, Ambassador? *Caresses Clyde.*

AMBASSADOR. Get your filthy talons off him, you disgusting whore!

Dragon Lady crosses to Ambassador, fiddling with hairpiece.
She attacks with hidden hypo. They struggle.

DRAGON LADY. Shoot, Blossom — shoot both of us! It would be worth it!

Ambassador stabs her with her own syringe.

Blossom — your greater victory will be my revenge! *Slowly falls, dies.*

AMBASSADOR. Clyde — disarm the girl!

CLYDE. No, dad. You'd kill her.

AMBASSADOR. *Calls.* Tran Dog!

Tran Dog enters.

Get her gun.

TRAN DOG. No, Mr. Junker. I do not work for you any more.

AMBASSADOR. What about your rice bowl?

TRAN DOG. Your rice was very bad. I got sick on it.

Blossom raises gun.

AMBASSADOR. Don't shoot — please! Look — I'm a powerful man. In my pocket, Clyde — traveller's checks. Take as much as you want! I'm a generous man — tell her, Clyde!

CLYDE. *Standing between gun and father.* He's — he's — he's exactly what you think he is! And I'm in the middle.

TRAN DOG. There is no middle — only two sides.

AMBASSADOR. I'm a human being. *Cowers.*

162

BLOSSOM. *Lowers gun.* If we kill you, they will only put another in your place. Our fight is with all of your kind, not just with one. The important thing is for your people to see who you are. Let's go.

CLYDE. Where are you taking him?

BLOSSOM. To show our peasants, whose villages he has destroyed, and your workers, whose sons he has taken, and the young people who are shooting his dope, to show them all who the real Mr. Big is!

AMBASSADOR. They'll never believe it: they're too stupid.

BLOSSOM. They get smarter every day. *Starts to march him off.*

CLYDE. Blossom. Can I come with you?

BLOSSOM. I hope so.

TRAN DOG. People in different countries are fighting one enemy. Some start early, others are slow to understand. But one day, all together, we will sweep him away.

Exeunt.

Trumpet plays 'Ballad of Ho Chi Minh.'

The San Francisco Mime Troupe

Presents

THE INDEPENDENT FEMALE

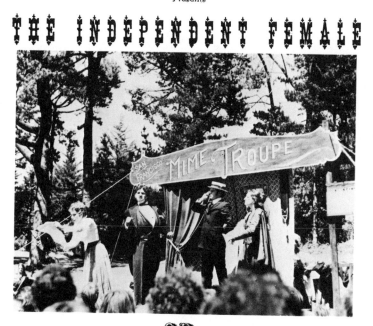

OR

A MAN HAS HIS PRIDE

A Melodrama

CHARACTERS

THE BARKER
MATILDA PENNYBANK. *Gloria's Mom*
GLORIA. *Her Daughter, Engaged to John*
JOHN HEARTRIGHT. *Junior Executive*
SARAH BULLITT. *Feminist*
WALTER PENNYBANK. *President of the Chamber of Commerce, Matilda's Former Husband, and Long-lost Father of Gloria*

Note: Opened May, 1970, at the Ash Grove, Los Angeles. Feminists had criticized, violently, a previous version in which the ironic portrayal of Sarah as the villain was maintained much more strictly, and Gloria surrendered at the end. This was the Mime Troupe's first experience of mass criticism. The rewritten version was an instant hit.

The Independent Female
or
A Man Has His Pride

INTRODUCTION.

BARKER.

Ladies and gentlemen. The San Francisco Mime Troupe proudly welcomes you to this evening's performance of: The Independent Female, or A Man Has His Pride. We humbly introduce you to the characters, and the themes, of this tender but passionate drama.

Characters enter as they are introduced.

Our heroine — the beautiful, innocent, but impressionable GLORIA. Will this fragile creature be led down the road to ruin, and parted forever from the manly, promising, and courageous JOHN? Or, will our hero save her in time? Will this young couple know the bliss that Gloria's MOM — to her eternal regret — willfully denied herself and her patient, long-suffering WALTER? Will this honest capitalist be reunited with the daughter he has never known? Or will the mad lust for power and the devilish plotting of the unspeakable SARAH BULLITT push everyone — even the City of San Francisco — over the brink of destruction?

Characters exeunt.

We hope all present find our story instructive, and are especially pleased that so many of the fair sex could be with us this evening. For it is in their interest — above all — to be reminded that:

In perfect trust, and mutual fondness twine
The mighty oak tree, and the clinging vine.
            Exits.

I

The Pennybank Home.
Mom enters.

MOM.

Today must be the happiest day of my life — except the
day Walter asked me to marry him, and the day little
Walter graduated from college. My daughter Gloria just
got engaged — and this engagement is extra special.
Gloria sometimes acts a bit — independent. I often
feared she might not have a future. But today it's all
settled — and her old Mom hasn't lived in vain.
            Gloria enters.
Darling — we must plan the wedding!

GLORIA. There may be no wedding — *Sobs.* We just had
our first fight!

MOM. TODAY? *Aside.* A bad sign. *To Gloria.* But why?

GLORIA. John doesn't want me to work!

MOM. The sweetheart! But what did you fight about?

GLORIA. I like working.

MOM. Gloria! What are you getting married for?

GLORIA. Because John is the most wonderful man in the world — deeply intelligent, and serious, and command-ing, and tall. But Mom — must a woman devote all her time to her marriage?

MOM. What else could she do? Oh — this might never have happened, had tragedy not obliged you to support us!

GLORIA. But, Mom...

MOM. I know. I know who keeps putting these wild ideas in your head — it's that ugly Sarah Bullitt — that career woman you've grown so fond of! She knows she'll never find a husband, so she can't bear to see you happy with a young prince like John!

GLORIA. Well, at least Sarah's nice to me! And John was so mean! Oh, Mommy — he yelled at me! He called me a...He called me a...He called me a...

MOM. Don't cry, dear — you'll get used to it. You see, darling, there is one thing education and modern home appliances and the pill can't change: and that's the basic difference between a man and a woman. A man has his pride. We may not be slaves in our homes any longer, but our main job is still to help our man feel strong.

GLORIA. Is that what you did with Dad?

MOM. I FAILED as a woman. And I don't want to see you make the same mistake, Gloria! You children didn't know this, but — I used to criticize Walter.

GLORIA. You don't think he just left because you got old?

MOM. No, darling — he HAD to leave, because I THREAT-ENED him. Don't suffer as I have! Tell John you've decided to give up your job. Be a woman, darling, before it's too late! Oh, my shame. *Exits.*

GLORIA. Poor Mom! Can I be headed down the same road? And is it true what she said about Sarah? Oh, I mustn't be so headstrong and selfish! I love John, and I want us to be happy! But this crazy independence — *The spirit takes her, and she begins a karate dance. Stops herself.* Sometimes it's stronger than I am! *Starts again. John enters behind her, gets a chop in the ribs.*

JOHN. So! You still think I don't make enough money!

GLORIA. I never said that — but my salary would help. But it's not just the money!

JOHN. I told you I would give you an allowance. Am I not enough for you, Gloria?

GLORIA. Darling, you're everything! But what about my job?

JOHN. What about it?

GLORIA. Mr. Peabody says he doesn't know how they'll replace me. He's so sweet — do you know what he said about our engagement? 'I hope this doesn't mean you'll be breaking up the team.'

JOHN. Gloria, once upon a time, not so long ago, man roamed the woods, hunting food, while woman stayed home and tended the fire. On the surface, things have changed since — but in his heart, man is still a hunter: at least I am, and I still want a woman in my cave!

GLORIA. Oh, John!

JOHN. I thought you were a real woman, Gloria — that's why I chose you for my wife. If you want a career, I won't stand in your way — but I want a wife, not a business partner. Goodbye.

GLORIA. No!

JOHN. A man has his pride.

GLORIA. *Aside.* Mom was right! *To John.* Wait, John — I'll do it — I'll quit! I'm going to make being your wife my full-time job!

JOHN. Little girl!

GLORIA. Forgive me, darling — I want us to have a good marriage — it's just that I've got the independence habit. *Chops him again.*

JOHN. I'll help you get over it! Lean on me, Gloria. I'm going to treat you the way my Dad said every woman ought to be treated: like the most precious thing a man owns.

171

Sarah enters.

SARAH. *Aside.* My only hope — in enemy hands! *To John and Gloria.* Good afternoon. Am I intruding?
  Mom peers around curtain, distressed to see Sarah.

JOHN. *Aside.* Sarah Bullitt — the company malcontent! I fear her ill influence on Gloria.

GLORIA. Sarah! I have some wonderful news!

JOHN. Miss Bullitt has some news of her own, I believe.

SARAH. I've been fired.

JOHN. Terminated, I understand, for insubordination.

SARAH. I said if they refused to promote me, I'd have to put a hex on the company.

GLORIA. It seems so unfair! Why, Sarah was the best

172

accountant the company had. And the least expensive. Don't feel too bad, dear — I guess a woman can't win. John and I are going to be married.

SARAH. *Aside.* Disaster! For her life, and our plot!

GLORIA. So I have decided to quit.

SARAH. Only last week, you said you'd never been so happy at work.

GLORIA. I know, but John would prefer that I stayed at home.

SARAH. So you're signing over your independence.

JOHN. You girls were made for the lighter work — washing, cooking, raising children.

SARAH. And you men for the heavy stuff — giving the orders. Why, men are so strong, they get paid for work we do.

JOHN. This bitterness is what makes your life difficult. If men have privileges, it's because we've earned them. After all, men are responsible for every major achievement of our civilization.

SARAH. Competition, pollution, inflation, waste, war —

GLORIA. What have we women done?

JOHN. Take Gloria, forever prattling about the way things SHOULD be. She needs me to stand between herself and reality. Why can't you be content to be what we need? Competent secretaries, thrifty housewives —

SARAH. *To Gloria.* What did you want to be?

GLORIA. A forest ranger.

> *John laughs heartily.*

What's so funny?

> *Mom enters.*

MOM. Why, Miss Bullitt! Quelle surprise!

SARAH. *Aside.* Uncle Mom!

MOM. *To Sarah.* What a lovely dress — it goes so well with your teeth.

SARAH. Thank you. Would you like a cigar?

MOM. *Ignoring this.* Well, three's a crowd, don't you all
think? So, John, you'll let Gloria help her Mom with the
tea?

JOHN. Good idea.

MOM. Come, dear. *To Sarah.* I'm so sorry you have to run
off — but I realize you can't be late for the Roller Derby.
Gloria and Mom exeunt.

JOHN. You're wasting your time trying to convert Gloria,
Miss Bullitt. She's a normal girl.

SARAH. *With heavy irony.* That's what I used to think, but
this news makes me wonder. Anyone can see how happy
she's going to be.

JOHN. She'll be happy if I can help it. But this must be
painful for you. I doubt there can be any happiness for
a woman who wishes she were a man.

SARAH. I doubt it myself — after all, what sort of woman
would want to be oversized and underdeveloped? It's
true that some women want justice.
Gloria enters.

JOHN. My hat!
Gloria gets it.

The only justice a woman needs is a man to shut her
mouth. *Grabs Gloria and kisses her.* I'll call when you have
time to see me. *To Sarah.* Do you know what the trouble
with you is? You're frustrated. *Exits.*

GLORIA. How can I hate the man I love?

SARAH. How can you marry that swine?

GLORIA. We're engaged! And you can just save your
breath, because I have accepted my role as a woman.

SARAH. To gratify, amuse, cushion, flatter, and serve.

GLORIA. We should let men be boss, since it means so
much more to them.

SARAH. To be seen as a piece of meat by every man who
walks by?

GLORIA. That's the price we pay for being attractive.

SARAH. You're preparing to spend your days as personal
   property. You'll end up with no life.
GLORIA. What's the choice: to end up lost, the way you
   are?
SARAH. We could have a choice, if women demanded their
   rights.
GLORIA. What rights?
SARAH. All the ones men have, plus a few of our own.
   What do you think would happen if all the women in
   our office went on strike?
GLORIA. Oh, Sarah — don't be silly. A strike in the office?
   That's impossible — those men don't know how to type!
   I mean the machines — the correspondence — the

phones... Well, I just can't imag — the whole thing
would just STOP!

SARAH. Divine vision — and women would be fighting
back! You've got to take my place: bring every woman
at Amalgamated out on strike for equal work with men,
equal work by men, and equal pay for equal work!

GLORIA. Equal pay? But wouldn't that be wrong? Are you
sure the company can afford it?

SARAH. Are you kidding? They own Argentina.

GLORIA. I could talk to the other girls — there's 100 of us
in our department, then 200 downstairs, then the whole
7th floor — golly, there must be 500 women in the
company.

SARAH. How many men?

GLORIA. Maybe 50 — let's do it! Oh, Sarah — equal pay, justice...

SARAH. Don't you think you'd better ask John first?

GLORIA. Oh, I don't have to: he's bound to find out! *Stops.* What mad passion stirs in me?

SARAH. The righteous rage of female rebellion! Let's get to work.

Exeunt.

II.1

A back room at the office, some weeks later.
Sarah enters.

SARAH.

'In education, in marriage, in everything disappointment is the lot of woman. It shall be the business of my life to deepen this disappointment in every woman's heart till she bows down to it no longer.' — Lucy Stone, 1855. Lucy was a revolutionary history has made anonymous. In history, the slaves never rebelled, the Indians died of shame, and all women ever wanted was the vote. But the irrepressible truth is that black resistance is as old as slavery, and there have been women fighting this country since men first established it; and what now is smoldering between the lines will soon break out and cover the page.

Our work proceeds swiftly — in a week Gloria had every woman in her office on fire — in two weeks the fever was sweeping the city. Today any laundromat may harbor an agitator — every steno pool may be a dangerous cell. But I'm worried about Gloria — she still wants her freedom AND her fiancé! That balancing act could topple our plans.

Gloria enters.

GLORIA. Equal pay! *Gives clenched fist salute.*

SARAH. Equal power! Let's hear your report.

GLORIA. Here's how the different departments line up. Accounting and billing are eager to move. Marketing only needs one more push to get started. The cafeteria girls are with us to a man.

Sarah winces.

But I'm having a little trouble in...Personnel.

SARAH. Personnel? But that's your own department.

GLORIA. And — John's.

SARAH. *Aside.* Gadzooks — it's just as I feared! *To Gloria.* He knows nothing?

GLORIA. Nothing. He still thinks I'm planning to quit. He thinks — oh, this makes me feel awful — he thinks we're planning a surprise for his birthday!

SARAH. Well, he's gonna get one. Gloria, if you want your independence, you're going to have to sacrifice your chains.

GLORIA. But what about love? I want to serve our cause, but that can't mean I mustn't love John!

SARAH. It doesn't mean you can't love, but you can't love your enemy. Very soon now, you'll have to make a choice.

GLORIA. No! I'll tell John everything! I'll make him understand!

SARAH. Tell him — but not until after tonight.

GLORIA. Our first open all-women's meeting!

SARAH. Seize the time. This very night we will call for a strike.

GLORIA. Strike!

SARAH. And it won't end at Amalgamated Corporate Life. The fire we light this evening will sweep the financial district. Business in San Francisco will grind to a halt — and it won't start up again until we change everything!

GLORIA. Everything? Oh, Sarah — you frighten me.

SARAH. Call in sick and go work on your speech. And remember — at all costs our plans must be secret.

GLORIA. At all costs! *Exits.*

SARAH. Hairy race of tyrants, your doom is nigh. *Exits.*

II.2

The Pennybank Home.
John knocks from offstage.
Mom enters, holding paper.

MOM.

Coming! Another paper — what can Gloria be up to? The way she banged in and out of here —

Another knock.

Oh, come in!

John enters.

Why, John!

JOHN. Good afternoon, Mrs. Pennybank. *Gives her his hat.* Is Gloria in?

MOM. Why, no. Shouldn't she be at work?

JOHN. She telephoned and said she was sick.

MOM. There must be some mistake. Why, I just can't imagine —

JOHN. Well, I can. Gloria's been acting very strange lately. She avoids me in the office. She's always whispering with the other girls. Today she — she missed my birthday. Her mind's not on me. There can be only one explanation. Mrs. Pennybank — who is the other man?

MOM. No...

JOHN. Your attempt to protect Gloria is short-sighted. Don't you see that her interest lies in my knowing everything?

MOM. Gloria doesn't confide in her Mom any more! I admit she's preoccupied — almost driven, sometimes: makes phone calls at all hours; comes and goes without warning...

JOHN. That's enough — farewell, Mrs. Pennybank. *Going.*

MOM. Wait — perhaps there's another explanation. *Shows paper.*

JOHN. What's that? It's in Gloria's hand!

MOM. She dropped this just now.

JOHN. *Grabs it, reads.* 'Are women human? Adored and ignored — last hired and first fired.' *Looks accusingly at Mom.*

MOM. I don't understand.

JOHN. I'm afraid I'm beginning to. *Reads.* 'When will women break the chains of slavery and assume their rightful place beside men in the life of the world?'

MOM. It doesn't sound like a love letter.

JOHN. It's much worse. Have you ever heard of Women's Liberation, Mrs. Pennybank?

MOM. You mean 'menstruation.' I've heard of it.

JOHN. 'Liberation' is the high-sounding term with which a clique of unwomanly, power-mad females masks its plot to destroy the family and enslave the male sex.

MOM. Gloria is a good girl! *Hands John his hat.*

JOHN. I know it — but one gone far astray.

MOM. I know who's at the bottom of this — Sarah Bullitt!

JOHN. Good thinking! *Returns hat.* There's no villainy of which she's incapable. *Reads.* There's another line — 'We meet here tonight.' Zounds — this makes it sound like a speech! Poor deluded Gloria is serving them as a carrier of the disease.

MOM. We must stop her.

JOHN. I mean to stop her — and when I bring her back she's going to need your constant attention. *Kisses Mom's hand.* Permit me to say, Mrs. Pennybank: this is what can happen when female 'independence' is not nipped in the bud. *Exits.*

MOM. Oh, I've failed again! Failed as a wife — failed as a mother! *Exits.*

II.3

The Office.
Sarah and Gloria enter.

SARAH.

At last the stage is set for our all-female revolution.

GLORIA. Oh, boy!

SARAH. It's only taken 10,000 years. Now to reach the meeting hall without being seen.

GLORIA. What we're about to do sets me tingling all over. My heavens, in a single month, how I have changed!

John enters, unseen.

JOHN. *Aside.* Something's afoot — aha!

SARAH. Remember — no one must see us.

JOHN. *Steps forward.* Feeling better, Gloria?

GLORIA. No — I feel worse.

SARAH. *Aside.* Meddling lout!

JOHN. You needn't sneak and lie anymore — I know all.

GLORIA. All? You know about the —

SARAH. Let him tell us what he knows.

JOHN. I know what a fool I was to allow you near Gloria — know what poison you've administered to her innocent mind — how you've provoked her to dissatisfaction; intoxicated her with insane ambition; hypnotized her into stirring up discontent!

SARAH. *To Gloria.* We're safe — he doesn't know about the strike!

JOHN. Thank God this is not going any further. *Seizes Gloria.* Listen, darling — it's all a lie! It's a plot against our happiness! Don't you want children?

GLORIA. Oh, John — happy birthday.

SARAH. *Takes Gloria's arm.* Yes, happy returns — now you'll have to excuse us.

JOHN. Don't touch her!

SARAH. Gloria's not your property yet!

JOHN. Be very careful. There are laws to take care of people like you — new ones every day!

SARAH. 'We are not bound to obey laws in which we have no representation.' — Abigail Adams, 1776.

JOHN. Darling, forget this woman — let me take you home now!

GLORIA. I can't — tomorrow I'll explain!

JOHN. Tomorrow! Do you think I could live through the night?

GLORIA. Please, John — what I'm doing is for us! It's for all men and women!

JOHN. Gloria, the male spirit shrivels when deprived of the confidence, the trust, of the female. I tell you this thing is wrong — you scoff at my words! Of course you can't know how you're hurting me — but I'll have to break off our engagement.

GLORIA. No!

JOHN. Then come home with me now.

GLORIA. Oh!

SARAH. Gloria!

JOHN. My darling, my angel, my sweet — is this the end, or only the beginning?

GLORIA. It's — the — beginning.

SARAH. And the end of your independence.

The word casts its spell. Gloria karate chops John.

JOHN. My God! Can it be hopeless?

SARAH. Precisely — it's hopeless for you. Women will soon be moving as one, and men will either move over — or go under, and learn for yourselves what it is to be kept for pleasure and breeding.

Exeunt, Sarah helping Gloria.

JOHN. Hideous affliction! But if it's too late to save Gloria, what must I do to spare others the same fate?

Mom enters.

MOM. John!

JOHN. Mrs. Pennybank! You, here!

MOM. I've found another paper. *Hands it to him.*

JOHN. *Reads.* 'Strike meeting at eight o'clock.' 'Strike meeting' — oh, no! What hellish vision rises before me?

MOM. It's ten to eight now.

JOHN. After you — we haven't a moment to lose!

Exeunt.

II.4

A hall.
Sarah enters.

SARAH.

Welcome to the first meeting of the San Francisco
Women's Union. I'm glad to see so many of you
here. Now I'd like to introduce our speaker: our sister
from Amalgamated Corporate Life, Gloria Pennybank!
Gloria enters with soapbox, stands on it.

GLORIA. My sisters! We're here to decide whether women
are human. Men struggle to make themselves more than
they are — women struggle to make themselves less. I'm
not just talking about the housewife who works a
16-hour day for what she can beg from her husband —
I'm talking about every woman who thinks she's less
than a man, and we all know that's every woman here,
regardless of how much she's paid, or how many token
privileges separate her from her sisters.

SARAH. Women aren't the only slaves in this country — a
few men own all the others. But all men oppress women
— even modern husbands who are happy to let their
wives work, so long as they do the housework at night —
picking out appropriate man in the audience — even you hip
ones who don't insist your old ladies be faithful, so long
as they take care of the kids. And how many women
know the simple facts of our plain economic oppression?
Our average wage is 50 percent of men's, and our share
gets smaller every year!

GLORIA. Tell us to get an education — a woman with a
college degree earns less than the average male high
school dropout! The only group that earns less than
white women is women who aren't white.

SARAH. A world where women are really equal would be a world with nobody on the bottom — because our egos don't shrivel if we're not on the top! But men aren't going to give us equality —

John and Mom enter.

so it's up to us — we've got to show the men that drive this machine where the power is that runs it!

JOHN. Gloria!

MOM. Come down!

GLORIA. That means — Strike!

SARAH. That means women say no! Stop typing, stop filing, stop serving, stop spending — start moving — until we have a society where no one needs to be dependent on one, because all are equally dependent on all.

GLORIA. Free our sisters!

SARAH. Free ourselves!

They lead audience in chant, then exeunt.

MOM. Shrill voices! Upraised fists! Anger is so unbecoming! For the first time in my life, I'm ashamed of my sex.

185

Oh, what would Gloria's father say if he knew about this?

John and Mom exeunt.

III

Not long after. Office of the Chamber of Commerce. Chanting offstage: 'Strike! Strike! Strike! Strike!' Walter enters.

WALTER.

Will they never stop? This is the worst pressure I've known in 35 years in management! *Bell rings.* Miss Jones! It's cost this city ten million dollars so far. Money that could have been spent on poverty programs, money that could have been spent to clean our polluted environment! *Bell rings again.* Miss Jones! Perhaps that's someone with the answer. *It rings again.* Miss Jones! *Again.* Miss Jo... Et tu, Miss Jones? Come in!

John enters, disheveled and desperate.

JOHN. Mr. President, sir? Forgive my appearance — I had to come through the sewers.

WALTER. What do you want?

JOHN. My name is John Heartright. Amalgamated Corporate Life.

They shake hands.

I — I know something that may help you deal with the strike. *Aside.* Gloria, forgive me — this is for your own good.

WALTER. Out with it, man!

JOHN. First — my idea is so extreme — I must know your plans.

WALTER. What harm is there, after all? Might as well have it out. They've got us, son. Business is paralyzed. Money's rotting in the banks — we can't move it. For the first time in my life, I can't make anything happen. They've got 100,000 women on strike! We got a call through to Los Angeles. Advertised for girls to fill these positions. A few old ladies in tennis shoes were all who turned up! And you can't put men in those jobs.

JOHN. Men wouldn't take them. This can't mean you're going to give in?

WALTER. Of course not. After all, we still own everything. 'Equal work' of course is out of the question — we'd end up without a clerical force. And 'free nurseries' — 'free transportation' — 'free phones' — next it will be 'free all political prisoners'! But that means we can't get around equal pay. We'll have to cut men's salaries.

JOHN. You couldn't cut — profits?

WALTER. You mean capital expansion? Are you suggesting we castrate the American eagle?

JOHN. Oh, no, sir! I wasn't thinking. *Bracing himself.* All right — I'm resolved!

WALTER. Let's hear it fast — their bargaining committee will be here any minute.
   John whispers to Walter.
   Bell rings.
Step into my inner office!
   John exits.
Come in.
   Music. Sarah and Gloria enter.
Good morning! Are you girls looking for work?

GLORIA. Equal work!

WALTER. So this is the bargaining committee.
   They offer to shake hands.
He takes Gloria's hand and kisses it. I've always been an admirer of women's movements. *To Gloria.* You look like a dangerous adversary! *Aside.* She would be, if we were alone!

187

SARAH. Spare us your compliments. You know our
demands.

WALTER. *Aside.* I'd hate to be alone with this one. *To Sarah
and Gloria.* Yes: 'free everything.' I find them excessive.
Management is prepared to make a generous offer.

GLORIA. Pretty generous, giving us what we've already
won!

WALTER. Spunky — I like that! Our offer is prompted by
concern for the families. *Aside.* Where have I seen a face
like that before?

SARAH. *To Gloria.* It seems your appeal has reached
management.

GLORIA. Ugh — I hate older men!

WALTER. Who is tidying the home? Who is washing the
clothes, who is taking care of junior, while women are
out parading in the streets? Management doesn't think
any man should have to carry two jobs, so it is acting fast
to bring working women back to their posts.

GLORIA. We are waiting for your offer!

WALTER. I'm confident we can work out an agreement. But first meet the other half of management's team. *He lifts the curtain, revealing John holding a pistol to his temple.*

GLORIA. Oh, no!

SARAH. Curses — foiled again by this idiot!

JOHN. Gloria, please renounce your demands.

GLORIA. What does this mean?

WALTER. It means that at least one American boy is not a curlyheaded crybaby Communist!

SARAH. It means male supremacy is the foundation of capitalism.

JOHN. It means a man has his pride. I took a lot from you, Gloria. You challenged my masculine role — I forgave you; you flaunted your disregard for my will — I still loved you. Had you been content to attack me alone, God help me, you might have destroyed me; but when you threaten every red-blooded man in this country, when you attack the foundations of the American economy — that's when I come out fighting like a man. Either you sign this contract — *holds out paper* — or I blow my brains out.

SARAH. Tear it up. The gun's probably not loaded.

WALTER. Does she want to find out?

GLORIA. *Reads.* 'The San Francisco Women's Union hereby acknowledges its previous error in proclaiming the equality of the sexes. Henceforth our organization recognizes the supremacy of the male. In addition, its members agree to return to work at previous rates of pay.' *To John.* Why don't you shoot me?

JOHN. I couldn't.

GLORIA. But you're asking me to betray a hundred thousand women out there!

WALTER. What's a hundred thousand women, against one brave man who loves you? By God, if I still had some lead in my pencil…I'd do the same!

SARAH. Love — the tender trap to pacify women!

WALTER. *To John.* If you live, I'll see you get a raise to start a good life with her.

JOHN. *To Gloria.* I couldn't look you in the face if I weren't man enough to do this.

GLORIA. The man I love — or everything I've worked for!

SARAH. Choose — your master, or our independence!

> *All look at Gloria, but the word has no effect —*
> *she does not quiver.*

Tear it up!

GLORIA. I can't — love is stronger.

WALTER. Thank God — just sign here. *Holds paper for her.*

SARAH. Not so fast! *She has them covered with a .38.* Now — tear it up. *To John, who starts to raise his gun.* Drop that or I'll blow your hand off.

> *He drops it. Walter tears paper.*

Now, we're going to write a new statement — one that
puts the Women's Union at the head of every company
in San Francisco: equal work, equal pay, and equal
power.

WALTER. *Clutches chest.* Ooof — my wallet! *Feels for his
wallet.* No, here's my wallet — I think it's my heart!

SARAH. *Ignoring this.* But first we must arm our troops. Call
the commander of the National Guard. Tell him you're
sending 100,000 women over — tell him they're strikebreakers — ha ha — and tell him you want them armed.
Dare to win! Thus do we accomplish in minutes what I
thought it would take years to achieve! Go on — call!

JOHN. You can't do it, sir. It will mean revolution!

WALTER. The woman is crazy — she'll kill us!

SARAH. 'Where the broom does not reach, the dust will
not vanish of itself.' — Mao Tse-Tung.

WALTER. 'I don't understand these young people.' — Pat
Nixon, 1970.

SARAH. Make that call!

MOM. *Calls from offstage.* Gloria!

GLORIA. Mom?

Mom enters.

MOM. I have something to say.

WALTER. Matilda? And — *Looks at Gloria.* Oh, no! *Clutches
his heart.*

MOM. Walter!

WALTER. *Choking.* Matilda!

MOM. Walter.

WALTER. *Staggering.* Ma-til-da…

MOM. *As if emptying a gun.* Walter — Walter — Walter!
Each repetition provokes a new spasm in Walter.

WALTER. Argh — *Dies elaborately.*

GLORIA. Dad?

MOM. I thought if you two knew each other, things might
work out.

GLORIA. Now there's no one to sign anything.

SARAH. *Who has turned her back in disgust.* Even death's a male chauvinist!

JOHN. *Who has picked up his gun.* Truer than you think! *He shoots Sarah.*

Sarah falls.

GLORIA. *Catching her.* Sarah! Darling! Say something!

SARAH. My last curse — their own works will destroy them. And my epitaph: 'Shot in her back for refusing to live on it.' *Dies.*

JOHN. There's no fair play with pure evil.

MOM. I'm just glad it's all over.

JOHN. *Picks up phone.* Police Department? Give me the

chief. Hello, Al? Chamber of Commerce here. You can start moving those strikebreakers — we've got the thing beaten. What? Well, if there's going to be a bloodbath, let's get it over with. *Hangs up.*

MOM. Amen. You'd better thank your stars that a man has his pride.

JOHN. Let's go home, now, and remember what it means — *He looks at Sarah's dead body* — to be an independent female. *He starts toward Gloria.*

>*Gloria grabs Sarah's gun.*

GLORIA. Don't you come near me! You'd BETTER back off, because I'm not going home!

MOM. She's very upset.

JOHN. Darling — don't you love me?

GLORIA. I love my sisters! And my brothers, if I meet any! *Going.* I'm going out to join those women on strike — and we're going to keep on fighting until we win! And when we all have our independence, then we can all have our pride! Coming, Mom?

>*Mom hesitates, then tentatively at first, at last strongly, raises a clenched fist. Women exeunt.*
>*John freezes. Barker enters.*

BARKER. Will HEADSTRONG YOUTH's impetuous course be halted? *Motions in direction of women's exit.* Will MANKIND recover its pride? *Indicates John.* Will RESPONSIBLE LEADERSHIP withstand this assault? *Helps Walter up.* Or does the implacable, rebellious spirit of INDEPENDENT FEMALES —

>*Gloria and Mom enter. Gloria helps Sarah up.*

portend this society's ultimate collapse?

>*In the event that audience does not go wild here, Barker continues.*

Young ladies and gentlemen, the future lies in your hands.

>*All bow.*

STAGES OF THE STAGE

195

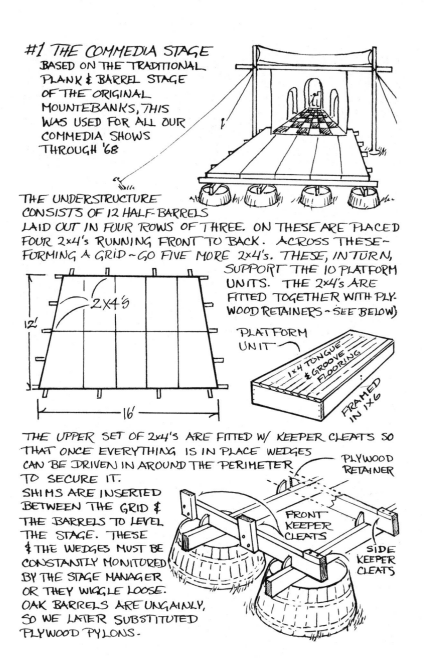

#1 THE COMMEDIA STAGE
BASED ON THE TRADITIONAL PLANK & BARREL STAGE OF THE ORIGINAL MOUNTEBANK'S, THIS WAS USED FOR ALL OUR COMMEDIA SHOWS THROUGH '68

THE UNDERSTRUCTURE CONSISTS OF 12 HALF-BARRELS LAID OUT IN FOUR ROWS OF THREE. ON THESE ARE PLACED FOUR 2x4's RUNNING FRONT TO BACK. ACROSS THESE— FORMING A GRID—GO FIVE MORE 2x4's. THESE, IN TURN, SUPPORT THE 10 PLATFORM UNITS. THE 2x4's ARE FITTED TOGETHER WITH PLYWOOD RETAINERS—SEE BELOW)

2x4'S

12'

16'

PLATFORM UNIT

1x4 TONGUE & GROOVE FLOORING

FRAMED IN 1x6

THE UPPER SET OF 2x4's ARE FITTED W/ KEEPER CLEATS SO THAT ONCE EVERYTHING IS IN PLACE WEDGES CAN BE DRIVEN IN AROUND THE PERIMETER TO SECURE IT.
SHIMS ARE INSERTED BETWEEN THE GRID & THE BARRELS TO LEVEL THE STAGE. THESE & THE WEDGES MUST BE CONSTANTLY MONITORED BY THE STAGE MANAGER OR THEY WIGGLE LOOSE. OAK BARRELS ARE UNGAINLY, SO WE LATER SUBSTITUTED PLYWOOD PYLONS.

PLYWOOD RETAINER

FRONT KEEPER CLEATS

SIDE KEEPER CLEATS

THE GOAL POST —

A SIMPLE CONTRAPTION FROM WHICH TO HANG THE DROP(S) AND THE SIGN.

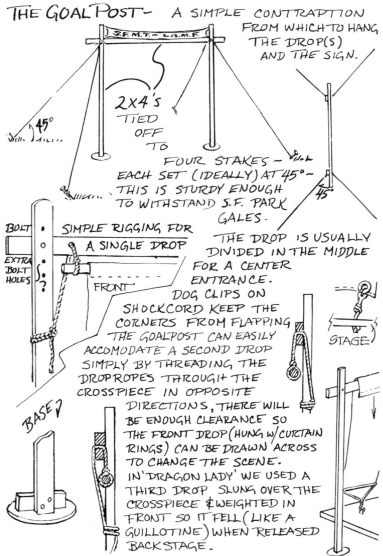

S.F.M.T. — L.A.M.F

2X4's TIED OFF TO FOUR STAKES — EACH SET (IDEALLY) AT 45° — THIS IS STURDY ENOUGH TO WITHSTAND S.F. PARK GALES.

45°

45°

BOLT

SIMPLE RIGGING FOR A SINGLE DROP

EXTRA BOLT HOLES

FRONT

BASE?

THE DROP IS USUALLY DIVIDED IN THE MIDDLE FOR A CENTER ENTRANCE. DOG CLIPS ON SHOCKCORD KEEP THE CORNERS FROM FLAPPING THE GOALPOST CAN EASILY ACCOMODATE A SECOND DROP SIMPLY BY THREADING THE DROP ROPES THROUGH THE CROSSPIECE IN OPPOSITE DIRECTIONS, THERE WILL BE ENOUGH CLEARANCE SO THE FRONT DROP (HUNG w/ CURTAIN RINGS) CAN BE DRAWN ACROSS TO CHANGE THE SCENE. IN 'DRAGON LADY' WE USED A THIRD DROP SLUNG OVER THE CROSSPIECE & WEIGHTED IN FRONT SO IT FELL (LIKE A GUILLOTINE) WHEN RELEASED BACKSTAGE.

STAGE

THE SIGN: IN THE OLD DAYS WE USED A BANNER STRETCHED BETWEEN THE TOPS OF THE UPRIGHTS. NOW A ¼" PLYWOOD SIGN DOES THE JOB ~ AND MASKS THE DROP RIGGING.

#2 THE FOLDING STAGE
USED FOR 'INDEPENDENT FEMALE'
AND 'DRAGON LADY'S REVENGE'

THIS IS A SMALLER & LIGHTER STAGE
EASIER TO TRANSPORT, TO CARRY,
& TO SET UP.

IT CONSISTS OF 6 PIECES:

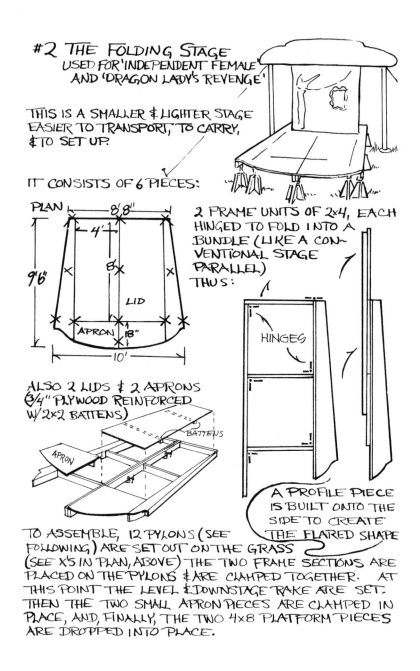

PLAN

8'8"

4'

9'6"

8'

LID

APRON   18"

10'

2 FRAME UNITS OF 2×4, EACH
HINGED TO FOLD INTO A
BUNDLE (LIKE A CON-
VENTIONAL STAGE
PARALLEL)
THUS:

HINGES

ALSO 2 LIDS & 2 APRONS
(3/4" PLYWOOD REINFORCED
W/ 2×2 BATTENS)

BATTENS

APRON

A PROFILE PIECE
IS BUILT ONTO THE
SIDE TO CREATE
THE FLARED SHAPE

TO ASSEMBLE, 12 PYLONS (SEE
FOLLOWING) ARE SET OUT ON THE GRASS
(SEE X'S IN PLAN, ABOVE) THE TWO FRAME SECTIONS ARE
PLACED ON THE PYLONS & ARE CLAMPED TOGETHER.   AT
THIS POINT THE LEVEL & DOWNSTAGE RAKE ARE SET.
THEN THE TWO SMALL APRON PIECES ARE CLAMPED IN
PLACE, AND, FINALLY, THE TWO 4×8 PLATFORM PIECES
ARE DROPPED INTO PLACE.

ALTHOUGH IT IS CONSIDERABLY SMALLER THAN THE
COMMEDIA STAGE, THIS SECOND STAGE STILL RE-
QUIRES 12 POINTS OF SUPPORT: UNDER EVERY
HINGE AND AT THE DOWNSTAGE
EXTREMITIES (SEE X's IN PLAN
~OPPOSITE PAGE)
OUR INNOVATION HERE WAS TO
USE SCREWJACKS ON A PYLON BASE.
THIS COMBINATION PROVIDES BOTH
STABILITY AND GREAT ADJUSTABILITY
(HENCE, ALMOST FOOLPROOF
LEVELING).

⅝ PLY

2×4

A PRIMITIVE
PYLON:

& AN ADVANCED ONE
(FOR USE WITH
SCREWJACKS)

CUT
2 OF
EACH

BOTH
BUILT
WITH ⅝" PLYWOOD

THE SCREWJACKS ARE ADJUSTABLE
SCAFFOLD FOOTINGS TURNED
UPSIDE DOWN. EACH ONE IS
BOLTED TO A WOOD BRACKET THAT
IS CUSTOM-FIT TO A PARTICULAR CORNER OF THE STAGE.
THE THREADED SHAFT SLIPS INTO THE CENTER OF
THE PYLON (THE PYLONS WILL LAST LONGER IF THE
CENTER IS REINFORCED W/A SLEEVE OF 1¼" CONDUIT
OR PIPE)

~THE SCREWJACKS ALSO PERMIT RAKING THE STAGE.

#3 THE WAFER STAGE:

THREE APPLICATIONS OF ONE ENGINEERING PRINCIPLE

FIRST~ THE 'SCANDALS' STAGE

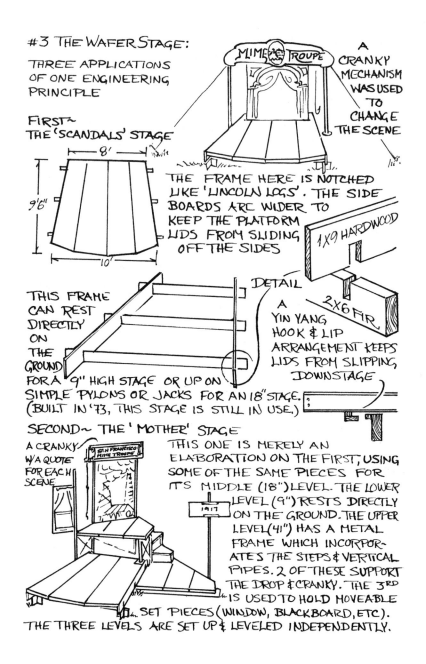

A CRANKY MECHANISM WAS USED TO CHANGE THE SCENE

THE FRAME HERE IS NOTCHED LIKE 'LINCOLN LOGS'. THE SIDE BOARDS ARE WIDER TO KEEP THE PLATFORM LIDS FROM SLIDING OFF THE SIDES

1X9 HARDWOOD

2X6 FIR

THIS FRAME CAN REST DIRECTLY ON THE GROUND

DETAIL

A YIN YANG HOOK & LIP ARRANGEMENT KEEPS LIDS FROM SLIPPING DOWNSTAGE

FOR A 9" HIGH STAGE OR UP ON SIMPLE PYLONS OR JACKS FOR AN 18" STAGE. (BUILT IN '73, THIS STAGE IS STILL IN USE.)

SECOND~ THE 'MOTHER' STAGE

A CRANKY W/A QUOTE FOR EACH SCENE

THIS ONE IS MERELY AN ELABORATION ON THE FIRST, USING SOME OF THE SAME PIECES FOR IT'S MIDDLE (18") LEVEL. THE LOWER LEVEL (9") RESTS DIRECTLY ON THE GROUND. THE UPPER LEVEL (41") HAS A METAL FRAME WHICH INCORPORATES THE STEPS & VERTICAL PIPES. 2 OF THESE SUPPORT THE DROP & CRANKY. THE 3RD IS USED TO HOLD MOVEABLE SET PIECES (WINDOW, BLACKBOARD, ETC). THE THREE LEVELS ARE SET UP & LEVELED INDEPENDENTLY.

THIRD~
THE 'FALSE PROMISES/
NOS ENGAÑARON'
STAGE

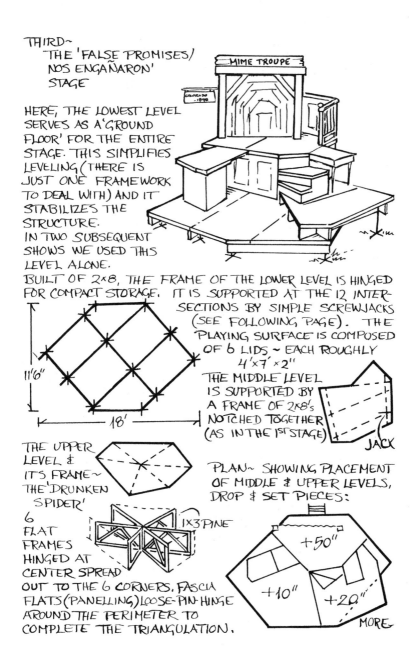

HERE, THE LOWEST LEVEL
SERVES AS A 'GROUND
FLOOR' FOR THE ENTIRE
STAGE. THIS SIMPLIFIES
LEVELING (THERE IS
JUST ONE FRAMEWORK
TO DEAL WITH) AND IT
STABILIZES THE
STRUCTURE.
IN TWO SUBSEQUENT
SHOWS WE USED THIS
LEVEL ALONE.
BUILT OF 2×8, THE FRAME OF THE LOWER LEVEL IS HINGED
FOR COMPACT STORAGE. IT IS SUPPORTED AT THE 12 INTER-
SECTIONS BY SIMPLE SCREWJACKS
(SEE FOLLOWING PAGE). THE
PLAYING SURFACE IS COMPOSED
OF 6 LIDS ~ EACH ROUGHLY
4'×7'×2"
THE MIDDLE LEVEL
IS SUPPORTED BY
A FRAME OF 2×8's
NOTCHED TOGETHER
(AS IN THE 1ST STAGE)

11'6"

18'

JACK

THE UPPER
LEVEL &
ITS FRAME~
THE 'DRUNKEN
SPIDER'

6
FLAT
FRAMES
HINGED AT
CENTER SPREAD
OUT TO THE 6 CORNERS. FASCIA
FLATS (PANELLING) LOOSE-PIN HINGE
AROUND THE PERIMETER TO
COMPLETE THE TRIANGULATION.

1×3 PINE

PLAN~ SHOWING PLACEMENT
OF MIDDLE & UPPER LEVELS,
DROP & SET PIECES:

+50"

+10"

+20"

MORE

DETAIL OF FRAMEWORK OF LOWER LEVEL

CROSS MEMBERS ARE SUPPORTED BY A SADDLE (2 HEAVY DUTY JOIST HANGERS WELDED TOGETHER) POSITIONED OVER A JACK. A NAIL THROUGH THE SIDE OF THE HANGER & INTO A HOLE IN THE CROSSMEMBER HOLDS IT ALL TOGETHER.

THE MAGIC OF 'VELCRO' A WONDER OF MODERN TECHNOLOGY ~ VELCRO STRIPS CEMENTED TO THE CORNERS OF THE LIDS & TO THE COR~ RESPONDING ENDS OF THE FRAME MEMBERS HOLD THE LIDS IN PLACE AND PREVENT ANY LATERAL SHIFTING OF THE FRAME ~ VERY STABLE ~ PACKS FLAT TOO!

3/4" CONCRETE FORM JACK CUT TO 10" & WELDED TO A BASE

THIS SIMPLE SCREW-JACK SIMPLY SLIPS INTO A 3/4" HOLE IN THE 2×8. IT PROVIDES 4" OF ADJUSTABILITY

THE AIRPLANE WING PRINCIPLE:

OUR STAGES MUST BE STRONG ENOUGH TO SUPPORT THE WEIGHT OF THE ENTIRE CAST, YET BE AS LIGHT AND PORTABLE AND COMPACT AS POSSIBLE. FOR THIS, WE HAVE DEVELOPED A STAGE CONSTRUCTION SYS~ TEM THAT WE CALL THE AIRPLANE WING.

IT IS BASED ON THE PRINCIPLE THAT STRUCTURAL STRENGTH IS DIRECTLY RELATED TO THE DISTANCE BETWEEN THE TOP & BOTTOM FACES. OUR 'AIRPLANE WING' CONSISTS OF 2 PLYWOOD SKINS SEPARATED BY STRUTS & SPACERS RATHER THAN BY SOLID WOOD ~ THUS:

3"

THIS UNIT HAS A STRUCTURAL STRENGTH CLOSE TO THAT OF A 3" PIECE OF LUMBER WITH A WEIGHT COMPARABLE TO A 1" PIECE OF PLYWOOD. AS LONG AS THE DISTANCE BETWEEN THE SKINS IS MAINTAINED (WITH GLUED-IN SPACERS) THE QUANTITY OF MAT~ ERIAL WITHIN IS IMMATERIAL.

THERE ARE SEVERAL WAYS THESE
'AIRPLANE WING' UNITS, OR 'WAFERS'
CAN BE BUILT. FOR 'SCANDALS' WE
BUILT THEM FROM SCRATCH
WITH FIR STRUTS BETWEEN
THE PLYWOOD SKINS AND SLICES
OF CARDBOARD TUBES GLUED
IN THE SPACES TO PREVENT
FLEXION OF THE SKINS.

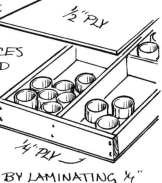

LATER WE ACHIEVED THE
SAME RESULTS

BY LAMINATING ¼"
PLY TO 1½" HEXCEL (CARD-
BOARD HONEYCOMB) SET-
TING IN FIR STRUTS AT
THE EDGES TO GIVE IT
SOME STRUCTURAL
INTEGRITY BEYOND THE
GLUE BOND.

A SLAB OF STYROFOAM
WILL ALSO WORK AS A CORE — AND
IT IS CHEAPER. HOWEVER, IT SEEMS TO BE
LESS DURABLE AND HAS A DEAD SOUND QUALITY.

THESE 'WAFERS' ARE PARTICULARLY USEFUL IN
CONNECTION WITH A RELATED APPLICATION OF THE
PRINCIPLE: THE ON-EDGE STRENGTH OF LUMBER
INCREASES WITH THE ON-EDGE DIMENSION.
THE FORMULA FOR THIS SECTION MODULE 'S' IS:

$$S = \frac{B \times H^2}{6}$$ WHERE 'H' IS THE HEIGHT
AND 'B' IS THE BASE

SO A 2×6 IS MORE THAN TWICE AS STRONG AS A
2×4. THUS, BY BUILDING OUR FRAMEWORK OF 2×6
(OR 2×8) WE CAN USE FEWER MEMBERS AND SPACE
THE GRID FURTHER (UP TO 6') SPANNING THE DIS-
TANCE WITH OUR WAFERS.
~ THE FOREGOING DRAWINGS ARE NOT TO SCALE ~
THESE DESIGNS ARE THE PRODUCT OF MANY
MINDS BOTH WITHIN & WITHOUT THE COLLECTIVE

THE CRANKY, OR PAPER MOVIE PROJECTOR

THE BASIC CRANKY CONSISTS OF A PAIR OF SPOOLS MOUNTED IN A WOODEN FRAME. THE 'FILM' CAN BE EITHER PAPER OR CLOTH (PAPER IS EASIER & CHEAPER; CLOTH, MORE DUR-ABLE.) THE CRANKY CAN BE MADE JUST ABOUT ANY SIZE, BUT TECHNICAL PROBLEMS (MOST NOTABLY SAG & WIND RESISTANCE) INCREASE ALONG WITH SIZE. THE PICTURES & WORDS MAY BE DRAWN TO BE PER-FORMED AS INDIVIDUAL FRAMES OR AS A CONTINUOUS FLOW OF ACTION.

PLAN YOUR CRANKY

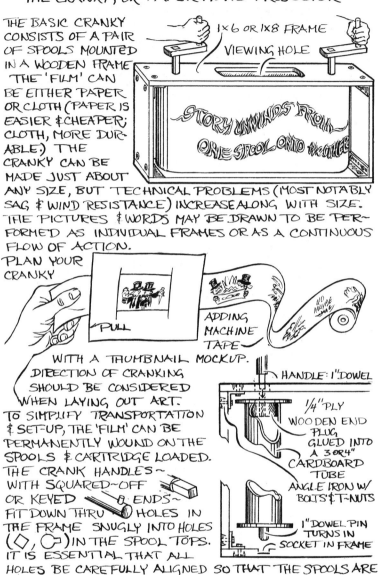

1×6 OR 1×8 FRAME

VIEWING HOLE

STORY UNWINDS FROM ONE SPOOL ONTO THE OTHER

PULL

ADDING MACHINE TAPE

WITH A THUMBNAIL MOCKUP. DIRECTION OF CRANKING SHOULD BE CONSIDERED WHEN LAYING OUT ART. TO SIMPLIFY TRANSPORTATION & SET-UP, THE 'FILM' CAN BE PERMANENTLY WOUND ON THE SPOOLS & CARTRIDGE LOADED. THE CRANK HANDLES ~ WITH SQUARED-OFF OR KEYED ENDS ~ FIT DOWN THRU HOLES IN THE FRAME SNUGLY INTO HOLES (◇, ⊖) IN THE SPOOL TOPS. IT IS ESSENTIAL THAT ALL HOLES BE CAREFULLY ALIGNED SO THAT THE SPOOLS ARE PLUMB & PARALLEL ~ OR THE 'FILM' WILL SAG, BUNCH & TEAR.

HANDLE: 1" DOWEL

¼" PLY WOODEN END PLUG GLUED INTO A 3 OR 4" CARDBOARD TUBE

ANGLE IRON W/ BOLTS & T-NUTS

1" DOWEL PIN TURNS IN SOCKET IN FRAME

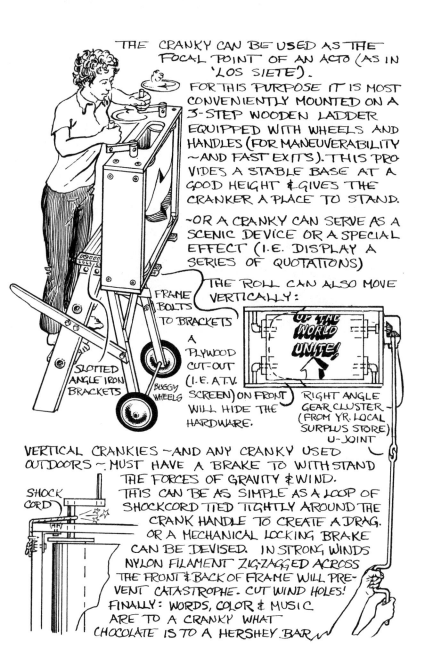

THE CRANKY CAN BE USED AS THE FOCAL POINT OF AN ACTO (AS IN 'LOS SIETE').

FOR THIS PURPOSE IT IS MOST CONVENIENTLY MOUNTED ON A 3-STEP WOODEN LADDER EQUIPPED WITH WHEELS AND HANDLES (FOR MANEUVERABILITY ~AND FAST EXITS). THIS PROVIDES A STABLE BASE AT A GOOD HEIGHT & GIVES THE CRANKER A PLACE TO STAND.

~OR A CRANKY CAN SERVE AS A SCENIC DEVICE OR A SPECIAL EFFECT (I.E. DISPLAY A SERIES OF QUOTATIONS)

THE ROLL CAN ALSO MOVE VERTICALLY:

FRAME BOLTS TO BRACKETS

A PLYWOOD CUT-OUT (I.E. A T.V. SCREEN) ON FRONT WILL HIDE THE HARDWARE.

SLOTTED ANGLE IRON BRACKETS

BUGGY WHEELS

UP THE WORLD UNITE!

RIGHT ANGLE GEAR CLUSTER ~ (FROM YR. LOCAL SURPLUS STORE)
U-JOINT

VERTICAL CRANKIES ~AND ANY CRANKY USED OUTDOORS ~ MUST HAVE A BRAKE TO WITHSTAND THE FORCES OF GRAVITY & WIND. THIS CAN BE AS SIMPLE AS A LOOP OF SHOCKCORD TIED TIGHTLY AROUND THE CRANK HANDLE TO CREATE A DRAG. OR A MECHANICAL LOCKING BRAKE CAN BE DEVISED. IN STRONG WINDS NYLON FILAMENT ZIGZAGGED ACROSS THE FRONT & BACK OF FRAME WILL PREVENT CATASTROPHE. CUT WIND HOLES! FINALLY: WORDS, COLOR & MUSIC ARE TO A CRANKY WHAT CHOCOLATE IS TO A HERSHEY BAR

SHOCK CORD

FOUR ACTOS

CHARACTERS

PEPE PEREZ. *A Peasant*
CONCHITA. *His Wife*
PATRÓN. *A Landlord*
EARL BUNZ. *Representing U.S. Agribusiness*
HENRY KISSINGER
PHYLLIS PORRIDGE. *An Unemployed Consumer*
HARRY. *Her Husband*
ASSORTED HAMBURGER EATERS
A WESTERN UNION MAN
A WAITER

Note: Frijoles opened in May, 1975, at a Rally for Jobs in San Francisco's Civic Center. Earl Butz, Secretary of Agriculture under Nixon and Ford, was previously a director of Ralston-Purina, the world's largest producer of pet and livestock food, which also owned 580 restaurants (including Jack-in-the-Box and fried chicken shacks in Spain and Guatemala) and food factories, feed mills, fisheries and hatcheries in Brazil, Chile, Colombia, El Salvador, Mexico and Nicaragua. Butz was forced to resign after making the following remark: 'All the coloreds care about is a tight pussy, loose shoes, and a warm place to shit.'

Frijoles
or
Beans to You

I.

Bananaland.
Pepe enters, sings, to tune of
'Chiquita Banana Song,' sort of.

PEPE.

If you want a vacation in a place that's nice
Come visit our tropical paradise.
  The climate is perfect, the land is rich,
  The landlord he work me like a son of a bitch.
    Bananas ripen in a patch so green,
    The sea is sparkling, the sand is clean,
    The government preserves all the ancient traditions —
    Poverty, disease, and malnutrition.
Spoken. But I'm not complaining — everything in our country is beautiful, except our life. The Yankees and the landlords bleed us so dry, the mosquitos are dying of thirst. We'd starve to death if it wasn't for my wife's little bean patch and the fish I catch down at the beach. And speaking of my wife —
    Crash, bang, boom, offstage.
— that's my wife.
    Conchita enters.
CONCHITA. Papas! Camarones! Hijos de la tostada!
PEPE. Conchita, my chile flower. Is anything wrong?
CONCHITA. Wrong? Oh, no — everything is just fine. Except I just heard down at the market, where I went to buy one chile and couldn't even afford one lousy pimiento, that that

209

fried shrimp, that fat shark, that thieving ladrón our landlord, has sold our fish to the Yankees to make pet food.

PEPE. Pet food! I told you this was a dog's life.

CONCHITA. Wuf! Wuf!

PEPE. Do not fret over foolish rumors, my treasure. How can he sell the fish that swim free in the sea?

Patrón enters with sign,
'Private Property of Checkerboard Foods.'

PEPE. I had to ask.

PATRÓN. Pepe, mi buen amigo. And your wife is as lovely as ever. Muy buenos dias. *Nails up sign.*

PEPE & CONCHITA. Buenos dias, patrón.

PATRÓN. I hope this ELECTRIC FENCE,...

Electricity noise: fence vibrates.

...is not in your way.

CONCHITA. In our way? That fence is gonna cost us our —

PEPE. Not at all, patrón. It's a beautiful fence. A brilliant idea. The only thing, it means the Yankees are going to get all the pearls.

PATRÓN. Pearls? Que pearls?

CONCHITA. Oh, just the little pearls we found in the clams on our beach.

PATRÓN. De veras?

PEPE. We was just going to get one to show you, patrón —

CONCHITA. But then we thought, a big dealer like our patrón —

PEPE. What would he want with a crummy few million pearls?

PATRÓN. Pinches gringos! They thought they could outsmart me all the time.

PEPE & CONCHITA. Sí, patrón.

PATRÓN. But you know where the pearls are?

PEPE & CONCHITA. Sí, patrón.

PATRÓN. And you're gonna show me!

PEPE & CONCHITA. Sí, patrón.

PATRÓN. Pues vamonos! *Grabs fence, gets shock.* Pinche fence! *Shoots it.*

Earl Bunz enters, singing.

EARL BUNZ. Oh, beautiful for spacious skies, for hamburgers and grain. *Spoken.* Buenos dias and howdy-doo.

PATRÓN. Oh, señor — these peasants were trying to steal the pearls from your clams!

EARL BUNZ. Easy, boy — pearls grow in oysters, not clams.

PATRÓN. *To Pepe and Conchita.* You're gonna pay for this.

EARL BUNZ. How do you like our new high-voltage fence?

CONCHITA. So you're the checkerboard square that put up that fence!

EARL BUNZ. Howdy, little lady.

CONCHITA. Why don't you get out of our country? He steals from us, you steal from him — we'd starve to death if it wasn't for this little patch of beans!

PATRÓN. Muy estimada señora. Your little bean patch is the very thing we came here to discuss.

PEPE. Well, we don't want to talk about it.

PATRÓN. It's fertile, well-watered, and sunny — the perfect spot for a nice grove of bananas.

CONCHITA. Bananas! We live on these beans!

PATRÓN. Be reasonable, señora — our country needs exports.

CONCHITA. What for?

PATRÓN. For the necessary things in life, like Cadillacs, hair dryers, color TV —

PEPE. We'd like to help, patrón, but we can't. Bananas don't appeal to me.

PATRÓN. Pepe, let's put it this way. Who owns the land?

PEPE & CONCHITA. You do, patrón.

PATRÓN. No, he does — and he wants bananas.

EARL BUNZ. Buenos dias, new employees of United States Agribusiness. Only yesterday, you were ignorant peasants, grubbing in the soil for a few beans. *Pulls up beans.*

PEPE. Now you want us to grub in the soil for no beans?

EARL BUNZ. Now you're modern workers — you're going to pay for your beans. There'll be no more sittin' around on your fannies playing marimbos or whatever the hell kind of music you people like. Work hard, and you'll be well paid — like American farmworkers. *Blows whistle.*

PATRÓN. Now get out there and cut them bananas.

PEPE & CONCHITA. Ho-o-ch —

  Patrón pulls gun, they start to exit, patrón turns away.
 — ptoo! *Exeunt.*

EARL BUNZ. Now, amigo, about those dairy cows we were discussing —

PATRÓN. *Wiping off spit.* I've come to the conclusion, señor, you are right. I'll replace them with beef herds. After all, who needs milk? Only the babies.

    Exeunt.

2.

Washington, D.C.
Music: 'Deutschland,' as Henry K. enters.

HENRY K.

Problems, problems, ach — have I got problems. The Russians got missiles, the Arabs got oil wells, the Vietnamese got Vietnam, and what do ve get? The shaft! Und does anybody care around here? Does anybody vorry except me? Vere is everybody? I got a plane to catch!

Music: 'Arkansas Traveller,' as Earl Bunz enters.

EARL BUNZ. Howdy, Henry.

HENRY K. Earl Bunz, the Secretary of Agriculture. You, I don't need.

EARL BUNZ. Easy, boy, you look as hopped up as a horny hoot owl.

HENRY K. I can't stand it. I'm supposed to be briefed for the World Food Conference. Und who shows up? A dumb farmer.

EARL BUNZ. Oh, yeah, I'm dumb all right. You remember the Russian Wheat Deal? That's how damn dumb I am. Lissen, Jewboy, I'm here to teach you the facts of life.

HENRY K. Facts, schmacts — I need excuses. The facts are that owing to the Vietnam War — vich I do not for one moment repudiate — the dollar is doomed, the balance of trade has tipped over, the Japanese have cornered our markets, the lousy Arabs are bleeding us dry. Vy? Ve got nothing to sell. It's embarrassing. How can I go to Rome without an ace up my sleeve?

EARL BUNZ. Henry, get a grip on yourself. Now, what is the one thing we got more of than anybody?

HENRY K. Problems, vat else?

EARL BUNZ. CORN.

HENRY K. Corn, schmorn. Who buys corn anymore? PORN, maybe.

EARL BUNZ. CORN, Henry — We grow half the world's crop. Meat — we raise a third. Wheat — a fifth. Soybeans — we grow 'em all. This is the food basket of the world, boy. Commodity numero uno — and we're throwing it away.

HENRY K. Vere?

EARL BUNZ. Down our own people's throats. They're eating it, Henry.

HENRY K. THEY'RE eating OUR food? You — schweinhunts! *Charges towards audience.*

EARL BUNZ. *Restrains him.* But they won't be for long. 'Cause you and me are gonna go to that conference and tell all those hungry nations we got food — TO SELL. Make us an offer. Then, watch that ol' balance of payments tip our way.

HENRY K. Not only the balance of payments, but the balance of POWER! Hungry people will eat whatever you put on the bargaining table. SELL food! That's brilliant! Vy didn't ve think of this before?

EARL BUNZ. 'Cause before, you didn't have a food company president as Secretary of Agriculture.

HENRY K. Zo. The food weapon! I can hardly wait to try it. Varm up the old Air Force One!

HENRY K. & EARL BUNZ. Rome, here we come! *Exeunt.*

3.

U.S.A.
Music: 'There's No Place Like Home.'
Phyllis Porridge enters with shopping bag, sings.

PHYLLIS.

Fly me to the moon and let me sit among the jars
Of jam and beets so overpriced this might as well be Mars.
In other words, what's for dinner?

[FRIJOLES]

In other words, where's the money?
Spoken. I'm not saying times are tough, but it took me three
hours to get through the express lane at the supermarket —
nobody could afford more than six items. Me, I could only
afford one. *Takes out can of beans.* I bought this brand on
account of the free trip to Europe contest on the back. I'd
love to travel — and I've never been farther than Vacaville.
Starts cooking. I don't mind for myself, so much — it's my
husband, Harry. He hates beans. He says they put him in a
Depression. He says it's not dinner unless there's meat on the
table.
    Music: 'Happy Days Are Here Again.'
In the old days, when Harry was working, I cooked pork
chops twice a week and steak every Sunday. Then Schlage
Lock moved to Thailand and Harry went on unemployment,
so I switched to hot dogs and hamburger. But last week was
the last week of Harry's fifth six-month extension. He's out
there looking for work now — but what chance is there when
you're over thirty-five? I think I'll turn the TV on and forget
my troubles. Maybe they'll have a good food commercial.
Hits TV.
    Earl Bunz on TV.
EARL BUNZ. Howdy, Mrs. America. This is Earl Bunz, your
    ever-lovin' Secretary of Agriculture, with a few answers to
    your everlastin' question...
PHYLLIS. 'Why are food prices so high?'
EARL BUNZ. Well, the dirty lousy Russians cheated us out of
    all our wheat. The Arabs embargoed our energy. And India
    and Africa, using famine as an excuse, are pawning their
    futures to gobble up all our grain.
PHYLLIS. So it's THEIR fault!
EARL BUNZ. Yep. These irresponsible countries who can't look
    after their own are taking the food right out of the mouths of
    our cattle. Your Department of Agriculture offers the follow-
    ing suggestion for those who find they cannot afford meat and

215

who have already tired of pet food: a variety of delicious and unusual dinners can be prepared from — BANANAS! *Displays one, and waves it under Phyllis' nose.* Think about that, Mrs. America — think about that real hard.

PHYLLIS. *Clicks off TV.* Bananas — ugh. I can smell them. *Sniffs.* Wait — that's not bananas: it smells more like — *sniff* — butch wax!

> *Music: 'Blue Suede Shoes.'*
> *Harry enters, grabs Phyllis.*

HARRY. *Bops & sings.*

One for the money

Two for the show,

Three to get ready, now go, girl, go

Spoken. Phyllis — I got a job! I'm in show business!

PHYLLIS. He's gone bananas!

HARRY. Phyllis, do you know who I am?

PHYLLIS. You're Harry — Harry Porridge!

HARRY. I am Jack.

PHYLLIS. Oh no — oh, my God —

HARRY. Jack of Jack-in-the-Box.

PHYLLIS. Oh. So why the weird outfit?

HARRY. Phyllis, you know those places don't hire nobody over

eighteen. But I fooled 'em, see? I got all dolled up and I went down there and I just kept moving. I outbopped 'em. They couldn't see the wrinkles.

PHYLLIS. Oh, Harry —

HARRY. *Looks in pot.* You can forget dinner, Phyllis — I'll just go straight on to bed. I'm gonna need all the sleep I can get. *Exits.*

PHYLLIS. Gee, Harry — at least it's a job. Hey, Harry — do you know why our lives are so crummy? It's all those people out there who want what we got. They're coming, Harry, they're swarming all over us. . . . *Exits.*

4.

Bananaland.
Pepe and Conchita enter, bent over, wiped out.

PEPE.

Well, it's Friday night. We're supposed to get paid.

CONCHITA. Ohh — bananas give me a backache.

PEPE. That doesn't matter now. You can buy yourself a new apron — I'm going to get me some fine shoes. We are gonna get a lot of money, 'cause we sure cut a lot of bananas.

CONCHITA. You know what I did? In the last bunch we cut, I slipped a note inside the banana. And in that note, I told the American who's going to eat it what that banana cost me.

PEPE. Cute, but dumb. They'll just think it's another throwaway wrapper.

Patrón enters, in pink Cadillac.

PATRÓN. Buenas noches, amigos. You like my new car?

CONCHITA. Sure we like it. Otherwise we wouldn't have bought it for you.

PATRÓN. Without bananas, none of this would have been possible. And now you get your pay. Let's see, you cut three tons of bananas, you make — *counting out eight bills* — eight dollars. Then there's the — *taking bills back one by one* — income tax, the thumb tax, the pension fund —

PEPE. What's that for?

PATRÓN. To build a beach resort, so I have someplace to go when I retire. So, with the usual deductions, you make: five dollars.

PEPE. You forgot to charge me for breathing.

PATRÓN. That's right. *Takes all.*

CONCHITA. Cute, but dumb.

PATRÓN. Señora, you also cut three tons of bananas, so before deductions you make five dollars.

CONCHITA. You mean eight!

PATRÓN. What is this? Women's Lip? You know you can't work as hard. So, with the usual deductions you make: two dollars. Now, my peasants, your pockets are bulging. But take my advice. Do not squander your money foolishly. Do not throw it away on luxuries you do not need.

CONCHITA. Just tell me where they sell the food.

PATRÓN. Food?

Band plays Safeway commercial:

'Since we're neighbors let's be friends.'
Se fue'.
            Shelf of junk food appears.
CONCHITA. *Spells out.* Ding-Dongs? Twinkies? Yukkies?
    Freekies?
PEPE. If you can't pronounce it, don't eat it. Where's the
    frijoles?
CONCHITA. *Reading.* Canned beans — five dollars! There's
    nothing here we can afford.
PATRÓN. Don't complain, my peasants. Look — no food lines,
    no ration cards. You are free campesinos, in a free economy.
CONCHITA. Yeah, free to starve.
PATRÓN. What have you been listening to? Radio Havana?
    Laughs, exits.
PEPE. How did he know that?
            Conchita shrugs.
    Conchita, when you can't eat where you're at — you have to
    follow the food.
CONCHITA. Huh?
PEPE. Bananas — the ONLY way to fly.
            Exeunt.

5.

*Punch Puppet (Harry) appears & sings,
to tune of Jack-in-the-Box commercial.*

HARRY.

C rank up the kids, jack up the car, to smack-in-the-box.'
            Phyllis enters.
PHYLLIS. I can't resist — I gotta see how Harry's doing on the
    job. And score a free burger. I think I'll surprise him.
            Motorcyclist pulls up, nearly hitting Phyllis.
MOTORCYCLIST. Gimme a Big Mac.

HARRY. A Big Mac! How'd you like a mouthful of knuckles?

MOTORCYCLIST. I mean a Jumbo Jack! *Gets burger & exits.*

PHYLLIS. I'll have a Jumbo Jack with fries, a side of onion rings, and a chocolate shake extra thick.

HARRY. Sorry, lady — we do not serve pedestrians. Next!
Drunk Driver enters, bumps Phyllis.

DRUNK DRIVER. Gimme a Jumbo Jack.

HARRY. How about a DT shake?

DRUNK DRIVER. Sounds great, I'll take three of 'em. *Gets order and exits.*

PHYLLIS. Harry, it's me — Phyllis!

HARRY. Phyllis! Honey, am I glad to see you. Boy, have I had a rotten day.

PHYLLIS. I brought you a Geritol.

HARRY. This is my wife — and I love her.
> *Welder enters in mask, bumps Phyllis.*
WELDER. Heebeejeebee eebee.
HARRY. Beejeebeedede?
WELDER. Hebejeebeede. *Gets order & exits.*
HARRY. They never stop coming.
PHYLLIS. Where else can people eat meat?
HARRY. Meat? I got news for you.
PHYLLIS. Never mind the news — just slip me a burger.
HARRY. I can't do it, Phyllis. Everything I eat comes off the paycheck.
PHYLLIS. Wow — how cheap can you get? But I'm STARVING, Harry — let's splurge.
HARRY. I ate two days' pay before I found out they were charging. I don't like it here, Phyllis.
PHYLLIS. Oh, Harry —
HARRY. I don't want to be a teenager again — not for a lousy two dollars an hour!
> *Earl Bunz enters, with gangster chauffeur.*
EARL BUNZ. I'll have a Jumbo Jack cooked medium rare, with butter — no mayonnaise — double lettuce, sauté the onions. I'd like a root beer shake slightly heated...
> *Chauffeur whispers to Earl Bunz.*
...and a side order of grapes.
HARRY. Whataya think this is, the St. Francis Hotel?
EARL BUNZ. Beat it, Vito.
> *Chauffeur exits.*
Aha! Do you know who I am?
HARRY. No, and I don't give a flying —
PHYLLIS. I know — you're Earl Bunz, the Secretary of Agriculture!
EARL BUNZ. AND President of Checkerboard Foods International, which happens to own this here hoof and mouth outlet. I'm making me a nationwide inspection tour, and I do believe I have found me a discourteous employee. Come out

of that box, boy. *Pulls him closer.* My God! How old are you, anyway?

HARRY. Twelve — but my mother fed me your hamburgers! You know your meat is so rotten the flies in here have halitosis?

EARL BUNZ. Come out here and say that!

HARRY. Come in here and make me!

EARL BUNZ. I'll do that, boy, I'll do that — and after I get finished putting you through the meat grinder, I'm going to have a word with that nearsighted manager!

> *They fight backstage as Phyllis freaks.*
> *Earl Bunz kicks Harry on.*

HARRY. It was a lousy job anyway.

PHYLLIS. Yeah, but now what are we gonna do? I don't know where our next meal is coming from — yes, I do. *Takes out banana.*

HARRY. A BANANA?

PHYLLIS. I bought this with my last dime on the way over. I was going to try a new recipe. *Peels it.* Harry...there's a note in this banana!

HARRY. Aah — another publicity gimmick.

> *They eat.*
> *Mystery music — Harry and Phyllis fade.*
> *Pepe and Conchita enter.*

PEPE & CONCHITA. *Sing, 'The Banana Song.'*

Help yourself to one nice banana
Ripened in our yellow sun
Feed your cows on our big fishes
Spawned in our blue-green sea
　　The same old sun shines down on your place
　　The same old sea comes up to your shore
　　How come some folks, they got nothing?
　　Some folks, they got more.
So help yourself to one nice banana
Meantime, we get thinner.

The land that was used to grow your dessert
Had formerly grown our dinner —
For you, banana is one small thing
You can buy it in a pinch
But somebody gets ripped off, you know
When somebody else gets rich.
    Is this what you want —
    The good life at our expense?
    No, we don't think so,
    We share the common experience.
    You work hard too,
    And still barely get by.
    We must ask why things are this way —
    Who wants it and why?
    Who wants things this way?
    Who wants things this way?
Mother Earth she want nobody hungry
She made plenty beans, bananas and fish.
But somebody gets ripped off, you know
When somebody else gets rich.
Yes, somebody gets ripped off, you know
When somebody else gets rich.

                Exeunt to music.

HARRY. What a banana!

PHYLLIS. Harry, wasn't that beautiful? 'We must ask why
things are this way — who wants it and why?'

HARRY. Made sense, too. A lotta meaning packed into a small
space.

PHYLLIS. Maybe it ISN'T their fault. Maybe —

              Western Union man enters.

WESTERN UNION MAN. Paging Harry and Phyllis Porridge! Are
you Harry and Phyllis Porridge?

PHYLLIS. Yes.

HARRY. No!

PHYLLIS. Maybe.

223

WESTERN UNION MAN. Congratulations — you have just won an all-expenses-paid trip — *hands them telegram* — to Rome! *Exits.*

PHYLLIS. We won! We won!

HARRY. Don't get so excited, Phyllis: it's only a trip to... Rome! *Faints.* Gotta go home — gotta get the Instamatic!

PHYLLIS. And my Gucci sneakers.

Exeunt, babbling.

6.

Rome
Music: 'Arrivaderci, Roma,' changing to
'Hernando's Hideaway.' Pepe and Conchita sneak
on behind large bunches of bananas.

CONCHITA.

I f only there'd been some food on that plane!

PEPE. Don't complain — you know it's no frills in freight. We must have been on that plane for twelve hours.

CONCHITA. Where are we, anyway? Look — it's a Coliseum!

PEPE. Must be Oakland!

Waiter enters.

WAITER. E! Vene qui! Subito, subito! Madonna — va fanciullo!

PEPE. Pastafazouli to you, too.

WAITER. Aiee. Bringa dem bananas over here. De banquet she's-a dis way!

CONCHITA. Did he say banquet?

PEPE. Let's go!

They rush off.

WAITER. Mama mia! Questi stranieri sonno teste di cazzo! *Exits.*

Harry and Phyllis enter with sore feet and camera.

PHYLLIS. *Sings.* 'Three coins in the fountain...'

HARRY. Hurry up, Phyllis. You don't wanta leave Rome

without seeing the Pope! What would your mother say?

PHYLLIS. I don't care, Harry. I don't want to see him. He's only going to ask why we don't have more children. Oh, Harry — I'd trade our whole fancy hotel suite with a view of Hadrian's Tomb for one lousy bowl of spaghetti with meat balls!

HARRY. They coulda told us 'all expenses' meant all except food. Hey, hold that — hold it right there. *Takes picture.*

Henry K. enters, bumps Phyllis.

Harry takes another picture.

HENRY K. Excuse me please — I'm in a hurry.

Harry keeps clicking.

No pictures! *Hides face, exits.*

PHYLLIS. Harry! Did you see who that was?

HARRY. No, but I got four pictures of him.

PHYLLIS. That was Henry Kissinger! There must be something BIG going on.

Sign appears: 'World Food Conference.'

FOOD conference — come on! *At exit.* Look at this menu!

HARRY. Divine — let's eat.

Exeunt.

7.

Music: 'Come, ye sons of art.'
Kissinger and Bunz parade on with soapbox.

HENRY K.
On box.

Welcome, distinguished delegates to the World Food Conference. Now that ve have all enjoyed our Veal Milanese, ve can dig into the very grave problem that faces us.

EARL BUNZ. Dig — grave — that's rich, Henry.

HENRY K. To eat, or not to eat — that is the question. Or more precisely, who is to eat, und who is not to eat.

EARL BUNZ. Tell it like it is, Hank!

HENRY K. A generation ago, most farms vere still owned by farmers. Most nations still produced their own food. Grain vas still raised vithout chemical fertilizers, und cattle vere still chomping on grass. Today, all these problems have been solved, leaving only the question of how to feed people.

Eastern music.

Pepe and Conchita enter, disguised in tablecloths.

EARL BUNZ. More delegates.

HENRY K. Who are you?

PEPE. *Severely.* Who am I?

CONCHITA. Who are you?

PEPE. I am my excellency, the Sultan of Muskrat and Almond, and this is her eminence, the Queen of Sheba.

EARL BUNZ. Muskrat? Wherezzat at?

HENRY K. I dunno — these emerging nations keep emerging so fast, who keeps up?

CONCHITA. Have we missed lunch? I simply couldn't eat what they served on the plane!

PEPE. It was fit for peasants.

HENRY K. *To Earl Bunz.* Call the vaiter.

Earl Bunz signals backstage.

If I may continue. At this very moment, hundreds of millions of persons are facing starvation.

PEPE. It's nearer than you think.

HENRY K. We believe that the responsibility of feeding these hungry millions rests squarely with the rich countries: countries that are powerful, that can impose their will, countries that enjoy an overabundance — of oil.

Earl Bunz applauds. Harry and Phyllis enter.

HARRY. Here's the conference — where's the food?

PHYLLIS. Sh-h-h!

HENRY K. Now, in case any of you found my message hard to swallow, here is our Secretary of Agriculture to shove it down your throats.

HARRY. Him!

PHYLLIS. This guy turns up every time anybody tries to eat!

EARL BUNZ. Howdy, folks — is anybody hungry?

Clamor.

HENRY K. Quiet!

Waiter enters with tray of food.

HARRY. Right over here!

Waiter starts to serve them.

PEPE. Waiter — that's OUR lunch!

Waiter snatches food back,
goes to Pepe and Conchita.

EARL BUNZ. Now, I know some of you came here looking for a free meal.

Clamor. Pepe and Conchita grab food off tray.

HENRY K. Order, please.

PHYLLIS. *To waiter.* Same thing they're having.

EARL BUNZ. But the United States is not going to invite the whole world to dinner.

Pepe and Conchita are stuffing food down
their clothes, and finally they grab the tray.

WAITER. Hey! *Grabs tray back.*

CONCHITA. I protest!

HARRY. That's right, waiter — now just bring it over here.

HENRY K. Just one moment — vat country do you represent?

HARRY. Lower Slobovia!

Tug of war with waiter.

WAITER. E basta! Aiuto! Sonno tutti pazzi!

HENRY K. Dumkopf! Get out of here! *Shoves waiter off.*

EARL BUNZ. As I was saying. The United States is in the trade business, not the aid business, so let's see if we can DO business. If you can't buy our food, or get your A-rab friends to buy it for you, why, check out our low-down-payment, easy-credit loans.

HENRY K. Step right up.

PEPE. I'll take a million tons of rice, six hundred shiploads of meat, and a whole shitload of beans.

PHYLLIS. That's OUR food he's talking about!

HENRY K. *Takes out order book*. Where would you like that delivered?

CONCHITA. Send it to our servants, Pepe and Conchita Perez, in Checkerboard Corners, Bananaland.

EARL BUNZ. Sounds fishy to me, Henry.

HENRY K. Shut up — can't you see this guy's an oil vell? Any veapons today? C-5As, F5Es, nuclear submarines?

PEPE. No thank you, I've already been helped.

HENRY K. *Aside*. Lousy Russians vork fast! *To Pepe*. Vill there be anything else?

PEPE. One more thing — any other countries here that need food, just step right up and charge it to the soul-tan.

EARL BUNZ. Hold on just a second —

CONCHITA. You want us to shut down the pipeline?

HENRY K. Vill you shut up? Orders, please.

EARL BUNZ. Lemme see your map, Henry.

PEPE. Who needs wheat here? Corn? Place your orders.

HARRY. Just a god-damn minute! *Grabs order book*.

HENRY K. Vat's going on here?

PHYLLIS. I'll tell you what's going on — you're over here selling the food out of our mouths, and back home he's telling me to eat bananas!

CONCHITA. What's wrong with bananas?

EARL BUNZ. Hold everything! *Waves map*. These people are phonies! Muskrat my eye. *Rips off disguises*. Looky here — peasants.

PEPE. Just give me back my fish and my beans.

PHYLLIS. Give me back my hot dogs and hamburgers!

Clamor.

HENRY K. Get back!

EARL BUNZ. Easy, Henry, let me handle this. Listen, boy — who buys the pet food that's made from your fish?

Harry and Phyllis cringe.

228

CONCHITA. So it's you, huh?

EARL BUNZ. Who lives on bananas so YOU can eat beef?

PEPE & CONCHITA. Us!

HARRY. We're Americans — we gotta have meat.

EARL BUNZ. Who pays for your camper and your electric tooth-brush? Who props up the American standard of living?

PEPE & CONCHITA. We do!

EARL BUNZ. And who wants to take away everything you got?

HARRY & PHYLLIS. Them!

EARL BUNZ. There's not enough to go around — so who's gonna get it?

PHYLLIS, HARRY, CONCHITA, PEPE. We are!

> *The two couples square off.*
> *Heavenly music: reprise of 'Banana Song.'*
> *The two couples hark.*

PHYLLIS. Wait! That's not what we want — the good life at their expense.

EARL BUNZ. You scared of this nigger, boy? He wants your job.

HARRY. Job? I don't have a job! You fired me, remember?

PEPE. Looks like we got some common experience.

> *All turn on Henry K. and Earl Bunz.*

HARRY. We're gonna make hamburger out of you, Bunz.

EARL BUNZ. Now wait just a minute.

HENRY K. Get away from him. Get out of the conference!

PHYLLIS. Get down off that pedestal!

Conchita and Phyllis grab him.

HENRY K. This can be negotiated! Let me go! *Appeals to audience.* Don't just sit there — Vy don't you help me? This is uncivilized! This is unbelievable. Let me go! If you don't let me go, I'll — I'll...

CONCHITA. You'll what?

HENRY K. I'll resign.

PHYLLIS & CONCHITA. You promise?

HENRY K. I varn you.

PHYLLIS & CONCHITA. It's a deal!

HENRY K. I varned you!

They kick him off and shake hands.

EARL BUNZ. Very touching. Working-class internationalism. How naive can you get. Do you people have any idea what life would be like if everybody had enough food? You'd all be eating beans.

HARRY. We'd all be eating.

CONCHITA, PEPE, PHYLLIS. That's right! We'd all be eating! Right on!

PEPE. Let's throw this clown on the trash-heap of history.

They grab him.

EARL BUNZ. Not the trash-heap —

CONCHITA, HARRY, PEPE, PHYLLIS. Yes, the trash-heap!

EARL BUNZ. Anything but the trash-heap!

They swing him.

CONCHITA, HARRY, PEPE, PHYLLIS. ANYTHING?

EARL BUNZ. Anything — but spare my life!

HARRY. I don't know, Earl — you might not want to live in OUR world.

EARL BUNZ. Why? What the hell are you going to do?

HARRY. Tell him, Phyllis.

PHYLLIS. Well, first we're going to bust the food monopolies.

EARL BUNZ. That's been tried. It's inefficient.

CONCHITA. Then we're going to get U.S. agribusiness out of the third world.

EARL BUNZ. Whew — I thought she was gonna say 'redistribute the land.'

PEPE. That too.

EARL BUNZ. Oh, no.

PEPE. And we're going to feed all the hungry people in the world.

HARRY. That's right! And we can do it, too.

EARL BUNZ. Feed all the hungry people — now I see your dirty lousy game. That's communism! You're all communists! Help! God! FBI! CIA! Waiter?

Waiter enters.

WAITER. You calleda, signore?

EARL BUNZ. Help me, boy. Do something!

WAITER. Ecco. I'm a worker, too. And the Uniteda States she'sa can't push Europa around any more! *Hits Bunz with red bat which he has hidden behind him.*

All congratulate each other, waiter exits. Bunz on floor.

PHYLLIS. This reminds me of a song!

HARRY. Oh, no.

PHYLLIS. *Sings.*

The same old sun shines down on your place
The same old sea comes up to your shore

CONCHITA, HARRY, PEPE, PHYLLIS.

How come some folks, they got nothing
Some folks, they got more.

CONCHITA. You mean you got the note?

PHYLLIS. You mean you sent it?

CONCHITA, HARRY, PEPE, PHYLLIS. *Sing.*

Mother earth she want nobody hungry
She made plenty beans, bananas, and fish,
But somebody gets ripped off, you know
When somebody else gets rich.

The end. Take a bow.

CHARACTERS

MYRTLE SLOTSKY. *A worker*
GONZALES. *A worker*
NORMAN. *A worker*
RICHARD. *A worker*
BETTY. *A worker*
ROSIE FINKELSTEIN. *A worker*
MR. BEAVER. *The Boss*
AN ANGEL

Note: Opened in May, 1972. This was the Mime Troupe's only successful attempt to find a dramatic use for juggling. The play was performed during Phase One of Nixon's New Economic Policy, the 'wage-price freeze,' when only wages stayed frozen.

232

Frozen Wages

The Factory, Monday morning.
Preset: a rack of seven juggling clubs.
Workers enter in pairs, telling jokes.

NORMAN.

Good morning, Rosella!

ROSIE. How you doing, hot shit?

NORMAN. Wanna go to the drive-in tonight? 'Rodan' is
   playing.

ROSIE. Sure! My husband's been wanting to see that show
   for a long time.

NORMAN. Great. We can take him along to wipe the steam
   off the windows.

ROSIE. Then he can wipe you off the windows, Romeo.
   Rips out his false chest hair.

NORMAN. Hey, baby — that's my chest hair. Don't be
   cruel!

     Rosie reads a Romance magazine. Beaver,
     the boss, enters and blows whistle. Workers
     start machine – passing clubs along the line.

BETTY. Hey, Rose, it's the Boss!

BEAVER. *Moving down the assembly line.* Good morning,
   Gonzales, Mrs. Slotsky, Norman, Finkel . . . WHERE'S
   FINKELSTEIN?

     Rosie is still reading as clubs pile up.

   FINKELSTEIN??!!

ROSIE. Yeeks!

BEAVER. Reading on the job! I'm gonna hafta dock you an hour's pay.

ROSIE. Couldn't I make it up, sir? I mean, I need my whole paycheck. I can barely make it as it is.

BEAVER. Then you shouldn't have been goofing off on company time.

NORMAN. Rosella didn't mean nothing by it. Why don't you give her a break, sir?

ROSIE. Why don't you give me a raise?

WORKERS. Yeah!

BEAVER. Why don't you all shut up and get back to work.

GONZALES. She's right, Boss man. We could all use a raise.

BEAVER. Raise? Why, we just had a raise.

BETTY. We did?

ROSIE. A raise in rents.

BEAVER. A raise in that cheap Asian competition. Kids, inflation is eating up my profits. I only made $150,000 last year.

WORKERS. Awww-ww-www.

    Fanfare. NEP Angel enters.

NEP ANGEL. Did I hear the cry of capital under stress?

WORKERS. Who are you?

NEP ANGEL. I am your government's New Economic
Policy.

GONZALES. Do you wanna take the rest of my paycheck?

RICHARD. Don't you think you should do something about
the environment?

ROSIE. Don't you think you should do something about
that outfit?

NEP ANGEL. Hark unto me, ye affluent and overfed employees! Our economy is in crisis!

ROSIE. So's mine.

NEP ANGEL. The gold is gone from the dollar. The balance
of trade has tipped over, and the goddamn Japanese
are mopping our faces in sake. Why? Your president
has sent me here to make one thing perfectly clear.

BEAVER. THEIR president? I thought he was MY president.

NEP ANGEL. Know ye that we in high places have sought
the cause of inflation, and we have found it right where
we were looking for it!

MYRTLE. High prices!

RICHARD. High profits!

NEP ANGEL. High WAGES!

WORKERS. What?

BEAVER. You heard her.

NEP ANGEL. High wages are the cause of inflation! Now you might have thought it was the other way around.
They nod.
Don't!

NORMAN. Hey, pretty mama. Don't you think the war might have something to do with it?

NEP ANGEL. YOU insisted on cars and homes and vacations. YOU had to have meat every night. And now you will be punished.

WORKERS. Arghghghg!

NEP ANGEL. PHASE ONE! I hereby declare ALL wages, and some prices, Frozen!

ROSIE. But-but-but...

NEP ANGEL. No buts! Return to your posts, proletarians. Any attempt to obtain a raise is henceforth illegal.

BEAVER. Tenhut! Dress right dress. Forward march. About face. Present arms.
Machine starts.

NEP ANGEL. I just love that military beat!

BEAVER. I like that part about frozen wages. But what do you mean freezing my prices?

NEP ANGEL. Pause and reflect. If prices are frozen, where are profits going to come from?

BEAVER. Duh...
NEP Angel indicates workers.
But I have to pay wages, don't I?

NEP ANGEL. Pay fewer wages. You'll be doing the economy a favor. Now pick an employee.

BEAVER. Johnson?

NEP ANGEL. Not that employee.

BEAVER. Gonzales. Get over here.
Gonzales comes over, holding club.

NEP ANGEL. Rejoice, modest minority member, for unto you it is given to go first down the road to your industry's salvation.

WORKERS. HEY, THAT'S GREAT!

GONZALES. Gee, thanks.

NEP ANGEL. You're fired.

GONZALES. Hey, boss, am I supposed to listen to this white tornado?

BEAVER. We're saving the company. You are now unemployed.

GONZALES. But, boss, I got five kids.

BEAVER. Got five kids? Start a Mariachi band.

> *Gonzales moves to side of stage,*
> *picks up sign, 'Unemployment.'*

BEAVER. *To workers.* He's a lazy Mexican. You guys got nothing to worry about.

ROSIE. Yeah, but Gonzales worked here for 10 years. Any one of us could be next.

BEAVER. Mrs. Finkelstein. Get over here.

> *Rosie comes to him.*

Shalom. You know, your people are very talented people: doctors, lawyers, tap dancers. There's only one thing wrong with them. They're all paranoid.

ROSIE. Get lost.

BEAVER. You're fired!

WORKERS. Fired?

NORMAN. *Raging; to the other workers.* Hold me back.

> *They hold him back.*

BETTY. Cool it, Norman!

NORMAN. *Cooling it.* Thanks, Big Betty, I needed that.

ROSIE. I got just two words for you, Mr. Simon Legree. Hoch-ptoo! *She spits, splits, picks up sign, 'Food Stamps,' joins Gonzales.*

RICHARD. Hey, you guys.

> *Workers huddle.*

BEAVER. Say, I'm a little worried. We might get into some trouble from the unions.

NEP ANGEL. When there aren't any jobs left, there won't

be any unions. *She pushes the workers back in line.* Let her rip!

Machine starts, four workers passing six clubs.

You see, there's nothing that can't be solved by more efficient management.

Clubs are dropping on the ground.

Beaver blows whistle. Machine stops.

BEAVER. What do you call this?

NEP ANGEL. A fuck-up. *She rearranges line.* Let her rip again.

Machine starts.

BEAVER. Splendid, marvelous…

NEP ANGEL. Your shop is going to be an example for the whole nation. Why, I imagine you'll be lionized, canonized, and written up in Fortune Magazine. *She notices the line has slowed down.* Why, whatever is the matter with them?

Machine stops.

BEAVER. What do you call that?

RICHARD. A slow-down. You wanna heat up our work rates, you better thaw out our wages.

BEAVER. *To NEP Angel.* Remember what you said. You said…

NEP ANGEL. Attention, Americans. Phase Two now begins. Your impartial Pay Board awaits your supplications.

RICHARD. We demand a cost of living increase.

BEAVER. I demand a cost of loafing increase.

NEP ANGEL. Loyal capitalist, since your case is one of grave hardship, we hereby grant you a price increase of 14 percent.

RICHARD. What about us?

NEP ANGEL. Toiling taxpayer, your prayers have been heard. They shall be answered. We'll let you know. Meanwhile, lag not at your labors.

Beaver blows whistle. Machine starts.

BEAVER. Hey, you're not going to give them a RAISE, are you?

NEP ANGEL. Honey, this is an election year, and we've gotta give something — TO THE ONES THAT ARE LEFT. *Beaver blows whistle. Machine stops.*

BEAVER. Mrs. Slotsky, Mrs. Johnson, get over here. I'm sorry, I'm going to have to lay both of you lovely ladies off permanently.

MYRTLE. Why us? You only pay us half a wage anyway.

BEAVER. That's why I have to fire both of you.

MYRTLE. Who's gonna pay for my groceries?

BEAVER. Get food stamps.

BETTY. Now wait a minute.

BEAVER. Get out!
Myrtle and Betty split, join Gonzales and Finkelstein, pick up sign, 'Welfare.'

NORMAN. Hey, man, you fired all the broads. No broads, no work!

RICHARD. Hey, look, man, there were six of us here, now there's only two of us. How do you expect...

NEP ANGEL. Boys, boys, please — look over there! *Points to signs.*

THE UNEMPLOYED. *Begging.* Spare change!

NORMAN. Sure, Mr. Beaver, just a little joke, you know.

BEAVER. Now get busy.
The two start to juggle all six clubs.

NEP ANGEL. Look at that. This must have been what it was like back on the old plantation. Tote that barge! Lift that bale!

BEAVER. You're terrific, Angel Puss!

NEP ANGEL. You're just a silly old thing! But I can't take the credit. It was The President. He's so brilliant! Think...Phase One, the Freeze — scare the piss out of everybody and start laying off workers. Phase Two, the Board — give a little break here and there and keep

laying off workers. Now, there's only one step left!
Beaver blows whistle. Machine stops.
NEP ANGEL. Announcement! We now find our economy in the midst of a grave productivity crisis!
BEAVER. That's right. We've got to step up production or close down.
NORMAN. I'm not qualified to handle all this equipment.
RICHARD. We're already doing the work of six!
BEAVER. Do the work of seven!
RICHARD. What about our raise?
NEP ANGEL. Ahem...Hark! For I bring tidings of great joy. Your Pay Board as of this moment has agreed to raise your wages to the unbelievable sum of $2.20 an hour!
NORMAN. $2.20 an hour?
RICHARD. I don't believe it!
BEAVER. Now get busy! *Hands workers extra club and blows whistle.*
    Machine starts. Two are now juggling seven clubs. To NEP Angel. Is this Phase Three?
NEP ANGEL. Hush, honey — it hasn't been announced yet.
    Norman and Richard keep juggling – then Norman flips out.
BEAVER. Norman, who told you to take a break?
RICHARD. He ain't taking a break — he's been hurt.
BEAVER. He's faking!
RICHARD. He's not faking — he's flipped out!
BEAVER. He's not flipped out...he's fired!
RICHARD. He's not fired, 'cause Norman and I are going out on strike! Right, Norman?
NORMAN. Son of a bitch!
BEAVER. You're not going on strike, you're fired!
    Richard picks up Norman, clobbers Boss with him & exeunt.
NEP ANGEL. Fire them! You don't need them anyway.

BEAVER. That's right. I don't need them anyway...wait a minute. I can't do the work myself.

NEP ANGEL. You don't have to. Attention, chronically unemployed!

BEAVER. Any of you workers need a job? I got one good job at $1.60 an hour.

Workers clamor for job.

ROSIE. *Interrupts.* Wait a minute...if I don't get this job, my old man will kill me. So, I'll take it for $1.50.

Workers clamor anew. Bidding increases
in intensity, each worker underbidding the other
until Gonzales shouts.

GONZALES. I'll pay $10 for the job!

BEAVER. SOLD!!

GONZALES. Hey, hey, hey, I gotta job. Whaddya say, Myrtle?

ROSIE. Do you realize what you've just done?

GONZALES. Whaddya mean? I gotta wife, I got five kids and I gotta mortgage.

MYRTLE. You got $10?

GONZALES. Ay Dios Mio!

BEAVER. *To NEP Angel.* I'm with you in '72.

Beaver and NEP Angel exit.
Norman and Richard enter, on strike.

ROSIE. Eeek! Norman, what happened to you?

NORMAN. It ain't nothin', baby.

RICHARD. Nothin'? Nothin'! Look, due to the incredible technological complexity of the society we live in, our friend Norman here has flipped out. Say...you guys aren't looking for work here, are you?

WORKERS. Er, ah...

BETTY. Well, we gotta eat, too, y'know.

ROSIE. Yeah! And why should we do you mugs a favor?

NORMAN. You're right, baby. I should have stuck up for you guys in the first place.

Beaver and NEP Angel enter with twelve clubs.

BEAVER. Gonzales!

RICHARD. Say, if we don't stick together now, these speed-freak wage-freezers are gonna squeeze us all out of work.

NEP ANGEL. Mr. Gonzales, full employment awaits you.

WORKERS. On strike!

BEAVER. Hey, Gonzales, you're not with these rabble-rousers, are you?

GONZALES. Sorry, boss. You couldn't pay me to work for you. *Gives the fist.*

BEAVER. What are we going to do now, Angel Puss?

NEP ANGEL. Why, we'll just appeal to the masses!

WORKERS. ON STRIKE!
> *Beaver and NEP Angel mime offering work*
> *to audience.*

BEAVER. *Demonstrating.* It's very simple, really — you just pass it along the line.
> *Beaver inadvertently passes clubs to workers,*
> *who juggle them, fencing Beaver*
> *and NEP Angel in with flying clubs.*

Now, you workers put that equipment down or I'll call the Tac Squad.

RICHARD. You're not calling anybody.

NEP ANGEL. Violence never solved anything. You're only digging your own graves.

BETTY. Bullshit! We're digging YOUR grave!

BEAVER. You workers put that equipment away and I'll do anything.

WORKERS. Anything?

GONZALES & BETTY. Get a job!

BEAVER & NEP ANGEL. *On their knees.* Wahhh!

WORKERS. *Raising clubs.* Phase Four.
> *Exeunt all.*

CHARACTERS
COMMUTER
BART. *Bay Area Rapid Transit*

Note: Opened June, 1970. Los Siete were seven Latino youths accused of killing a San Francisco policeman. One was never captured; six stood trial in 1970. After seven months of testimony in a courtroom packed with their supporters, all were acquitted. BART, the Bay Area Rapid Transit System, then under construction, opened in 1973. The downtown buildings depicted on the cranky were figments of the artists' imagination at the time; they have since been built. The Cranky, a device for showing a paper movie, is shown on pages 204-205.

Los Siete

Commuter enters in suit with attaché case.
Time: 1976*

COMMUTER.

B oy, oh boy! I can hardly wait — my first subway ride! Just think — BART! It's finally here! Gosh, just like New York. Would ya believe it? Oops — here it comes! God, it's really big.

BART enters, in silver cape, helmet and sunglasses.
He wheels out silver Cranky.

BART. Hi there — my name is BART, and I'm here to serve you. Where would you like to go?

COMMUTER. To the Mission District — Twenty-fourth Street.

BART. Welcome aboard. As we proceed you are invited to enjoy the educational murals which line the walls of my tunnel. And I, BART, will attempt to add to your enjoyment by a running commentary on the points of interest. I am also programmed to answer any simple questions you may have. Is that clear?

COMMUTER. Huh? Yeah, sure.... This is really out of sight.

BART. Relax, my friend. And always remember, BART is only the beginning. *Starts Cranky.* What we see at the outset of the Mural of Progress is the San Francisco of Yesteryear — charming, fascinating, the financial capital of the West Coast, but somehow still provincial, low profile. Oh, it has its towers of commerce, but it lacks executive living quarters for the young movers and shakers of high finance. They're

---

*This play, written in 1970, was set in the future.

The San Francisco of yesteryear.

forced to live in faraway suburbs, and so eventually their businesses move there too and the inner city decays. A tragic situation; but with the coming of me, BART, new high-rise luxury apartments — the Dolores Towers, the Bernal Arms, the hanging gardens of Guerrero — sprout like magic castles in districts where nobody worth mentioning had lived for years. Like sequoias from garbage heaps, the new Manhattan rises from the slums.

COMMUTER. Boy, that's progress all right. I live in one of those places, too — forty-second floor of the Valencia Vista View. This sure is a nice city. And I like my job, too. It's ...

The inner city decays.

A new Manhattan rises from the slums.

BART. Simple questions only! All this was not achieved without sacrifice and struggle. There were those who attempted to halt San Francisco's progress, out of base and antisocial motives.

COMMUTER. Eek! What are those ugly things?

BART. Those, dear patron, are the former inhabitants of the Mission District. They were known as Latinos. Please do not misunderstand. Your BART system has absolutely nothing against persons of the Hispano-American persuasion. As you may know, we employ more than our quota of them in responsible positions.

We employ more than our quota of them in responsible positions.

COMMUTER. Oh, he looks nice.

BART. They are a perfectly nice people. But as the executive director of our Urban Redevelopment Agency, M. Justin Herman, once remarked: 'They simply can't afford to live in San Francisco.'

COMMUTER. I can understand that — my place isn't so cheap either. Why, do you know what I have to pay for three little rooms and...

BART. What did I just say?

COMMUTER. Simple questions only.

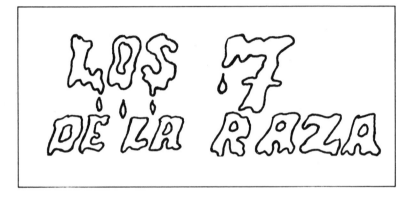

BART. Now, living where you can't afford to live creates many dangerous anxieties and illusions and often leads to violence in the streets.

COMMUTER. I'm against that.

BART. Of course you are. And where you live, there isn't any. But once upon a time there WAS violence in the Mission District — and the ringleaders of it were the notorious Los Siete de la Raza.

COMMUTER. I never heard of it.

BART. Of course not. You can thank responsible journalism for that.

COMMUTER. Was it something like the Mafia?

BART. The what?

COMMUTER. The Mafia?

BART. There is no Mafia in San Francisco. The only organized crime in San Francisco is the Breakfast for Children program. No — the Los Siete gang was a bunch of COMMUNITY ORGANIZERS — or, as our colorful Mayor Alioto put it, PUNKS. This is the story of seven punks in the Mission District and how they stood in the way of progress.

COMMUTER. You mean they didn't want BART?

BART. First things first! These seven Latin hippie types made a

They didn't think much of our high schools.

lot of noise in the Mission District once upon a time. Seems they didn't think much of our high schools. So what did they do? Set up their own so-called college readiness program. Well, you can imagine what that led to!

COMMUTER. Latins going to college?

BART. Exactly — a senseless, cowardly attack on the American system of higher education.

COMMUTER. But isn't everyone supposed to go to college?

BART. Of course not, stupid. If everyone went to college, who'd pacify Cambodia? Why do you think we have a tracking system?

COMMUTER. A what?

BART. A TRACKING SYSTEM, my dense friend. For example, by the time you were ten years old, you were already college material; by the time those people in the Mission were ten, they could hardly speak English. That's the way it is.

COMMUTER. But it's not their fault!

BART. Well, it's certainly not MY fault. Is it your fault?

COMMUTER. No... I guess not...

BART. Say it loud! It's not my fault!

COMMUTER. It's — it's not my fault!

BART. That's the American way. And now back to our story.
Now, college readiness was not all the notorious Los Siete
gang was guilty of. They were also spreading PROPAGANDA
against the city, against progress, against ME!

COMMUTER. Against YOU? But why!

BART. They spread the malicious rumor that the city government was merely waiting till I was installed before they
hiked the property taxes sky high and forced the Latin people out of the Mission District. And they dared to suggest
that the Latin people should ORGANIZE themselves not to let
that happen.

COMMUTER. But isn't that — wasn't that...

BART. Isn't that wasn't that WHAT?

COMMUTER. Sort of the way things — actually happened?

BART. All except for the organizing part, my friend, because we
stopped them in time!

COMMUTER. Oh — that's good. How did you stop them?

BART. Oh, my warmhearted passenger, if you have tears, pre-
pare to shed them now. Imagine, if you will, two selfless,
dedicated, sincere and muscular officers of the law. Two
men who heard themselves called pigs, and did not flinch,
but merely smiled and toyed with the rubber hoses in their
pockets.

Above all, go in disguise.

251

COMMUTER. I can really imagine them.

BART. Their assignment: 'Follow Los Siete. But above all, go in disguise: don't let them know you are policemen.' For naturally, they are cop-haters.

COMMUTER. Naturally.

BART. And then, one terrible day, they became cop-KILLERS too.

COMMUTER. Oh, my GOD!

BART. Yes. The two officers, firm in the line of duty, saw the sinister Los Siete actually carrying a TV set.

Shot with his partner's gun.

COMMUTER. Oh, my GOD!

BART. The officers naturally approached the surly youths for questioning. Let us not dwell on the lurid details. Suffice it to say that in the ensuing scuffle one of those brave, physically beautiful officers was shot in the heart with his partner's gun.

COMMUTER. Accidentally shot by his partner! That is tragic.

BART. Let me make one thing perfectly clear. The officer was shot, with his partner's gun, by Los Siete.

COMMUTER. Which one of 'em did it?

BART. All of 'em. We don't know how exactly, but we're work-

Which one of 'em did it? All of 'em.

ing on it. I shudder to think what they would've done if
they'd known he was a police officer.

COMMUTER. You mean they thought he was just a —

BART. Just a guy with a rubber hose and a bulge in his jacket,
after their TV set. And they wanted to go to college.

COMMUTER. What happened to them?

BART. Oh, they got away at first, but your police department
reacted swiftly, and in due time we got six of them. But our
story does not end here. As you know, I am the first BART
train to enter the Mission District, and today you will be
privileged to witness a special opening ceremony.

Your police department reacted swiftly.

253

COMMUTER. A ceremony?

BART. The Los Siete and their families and the twenty-nine Latinos who still live in the Mission District will be standing in the station as I arrive.

COMMUTER. In the station?

BART. On the tracks!

COMMUTER. I don't want to see that!

BART. Then close your eyes, you mashed potato!

COMMUTER. But I'll feel it!

BART. Too bad. How do you think you got your job, and your new high-rise luxury apartment?

COMMUTER. But I hate my job — AND my apartment — it looks like a vacuum cleaner. And so do you!

On the tracks.

Welcome to Daly City, end of the line.

BART. We are approaching the station — do you hear the people cheering?

COMMUTER. They're not cheering — they're screaming! Let me out!

BART. Too late! Life is short, BART is long! This is now the Daly City Express. You'll enjoy the new Daly City — it is now one building, sixty-seven square blocks! It also forms the northern border of the City of Los Angeles.

COMMUTER. Why didn't somebody fight this?

BART. Los Siete fought — but YOU wanted security. And now you've got security, courtesy of the Total State. Welcome to Daly City — end of the line.

    The Cranky ends in a blinding sheet of Mylar.

255

CHARACTERS
THE WORLD
ECO-MAN
GOVERNMENT MAN
PRIVATE ENTERPRISE MAN
POPULATION EXPERT

Note: Opened April, 1970, at a San Jose State College 'Survival Fair,' at which students protested the waste of our natural resources by burning a new car. This was around the time the word 'ecology' first came into currency.

Eco-Man

Woe is my lot and alas for my everything. I am the World, and I'm sick. My sweet golden breath has turned thick and yellow — behold, I exhale and it just sits there. My tender little ponds and rivulets are choked with scum. I got nothing to dress myself up in anymore except a crummy plastic tulip. O alas and goddamnit. Who is my enemy who poisons me in my innocence? Who stuffs up my cornucopia with excrement? Who is the shit? Man, that is who — the most ungrateful parasite that ever sucked my tit. And here he comes now.

Eco-Man enters.

ECO-MAN. GOOD morning, World, good old girl, it's a pleasure to look on you this morning.

WORLD. *Aside.* There he goes with his flattery again. *Aloud.* Oh really? You don't notice anything — different?

ECO-MAN. *Aside.* Let's face it, the old girl's had her day. *Aloud.* Why, no, World — you're looking fabulous. I don't know how you manage to age so gracefully. Oh and what a lovely tulip you're wearing. *Aside.* It almost fooled me for a minute.

WORLD. O Eco-Man, I have some bad news for you. I, your world, am dying.

ECO-MAN. Oh, come, come — you don't look THAT bad.

WORLD. I'm dying, Eco-Man — dying.

ECO-MAN. Nonsense, World, as planets go you're hardly out of your diapers.

WORLD. Eco-Man, we have 50 years left.

ECO-MAN. Er — did you say we?

WORLD. Oui.

ECO-MAN. Sacry blue! Why didn't you tell me this earlier?

WORLD. The symptoms didn't add up till just now. And the doctors say it may not even be 50 years, maybe 30, before I'm — a pile of bones.

ECO-MAN. Oh no!

WORLD. O Eco-Man, do you remember when I had roses in my cheeks?

ECO-MAN. Don't cry! Don't excite yourself! Here, sit down on your axis — don't get overheated. I'll report this to the proper authorities, they'll know what to do — I'll take care of it, believe me, you got nothing to worry about.

WORLD. *Lying down.* O Eco-Man, I hope you're right. But it has to be something drastic — there's so little time.

ECO-MAN. Put your trust in me, my environment — I won't let you perish. Adieu.

WORLD. Adieu and perhaps goodbye. *Swoons.*

ECO-MAN. O heavy information! There's no time to lose. Who shall I report it to? I know — the federal government! They're in charge of conservation — they're even bigger than the Sierra Club — THEY'LL know what to do. O Agency of my Government, I, Eco-Man, a taxpayer, request of thee some free information.

Government Man enters. Drunk, uniform, hip flask.

GOV'T MAN. O taxpayer Eco-Man, your federal government is responsive to your requests but I'm a very busy man. Make it snappy.

ECO-MAN. O guardian of my natural resources, I have spoken to the world and she is dying.

GOV'T MAN. O taxpayer Eco-Man, the federal government has

taken due note of your problem and calls to your attention the great efforts it is already making in the field of conversation, er, conservation. Next to the war in Vietnam and the war on poverty, the war on the environment is your government's very highest priority.

ECO-MAN. Wait a minute. If Vietnam is the highest — and you're spraying Vietnam with herbicides —

GOV'T MAN. And wiping out a million square miles of enemy territory. So what? I quote Secretary Laird: There are some issues more pressing than mere survival. Let's save the FREE world first.

ECO-MAN. But even in the free world we have to do something drastic.

GOV'T MAN. Drastic? Young fella, around here we do things through the law, under the law, of the law, by the law and for the law. That's the Thomas Jefferson Way!

ECO-MAN. Then — why don't you make laws against pollution?

GOV'T MAN. Already have, son. There've been drastic anti-pollution laws at the local, state, and federal levels for years and years.

ECO-MAN. There have? What a relief! It must be some job to enforce all those laws.

GOV'T MAN. You bet it is. Why, your federal government has gone so far as to fine Standard Oil Co. — that's THE Standard Oil Co. — a hundred dollars a day for breaking the anti-pollution laws.

ECO-MAN. *Appalled.* A hundred dollars a day? But they make over a billion dollars a year!

GOV'T MAN. I know. That's why the real force of the law resides in private enterprise, private initiative and private property: what we call the Private Parts.

World groans.

ECO-MAN. Listen, the world is in pain. Can't YOU do anything?

GOV'T MAN. Well, of course I'm not a medical man myself, but just offhand I'd say your little old world is suffering from a bad case of insurgent lice. A little spot of this green beret pesticide can't do any harm. *Applies it.*

World shrieks.

ECO-MAN. Stop, you're making it worse.

GOV'T MAN. Better sick than bolshevik. Best of luck, Eco-Man, and take my advice, leave politics to the specialists, your public servants. Have a toke? *Offers flask.*

ECO-MAN. No thanks.

GOV'T MAN. Pity, special forces in it. *Swigs.* Thanking you again for your interest, we remain, sincerely yours, comma. *Exits.*

ECO-MAN. Alack! The world is sinking fast! Her beaches are black with oil, her milk is radioactive! O fatal eco-crisis, who will save the world? Wait — who did he say? O Private Enterprise — I, Eco-Man, a consumer, appeal to your public relations division!

P. R. Man enters. Suit, big smile, clear plastic mask.

P. R. MAN. Hi there! Looking for something a little better? At capital growth we make a business of your problems! In fact, problems is our most important product.

ECO-MAN. O private enterprise! Thank God you're here... You can do anything! Help, the world is dying...it's an eco-crisis...we have to take drastic measures!

P. R. MAN. Is it really as bad as all that?

ECO-MAN. Yeah! We gotta STOP it, right now — if we don't, we'll all die!

P. R. MAN. Right! And private enterprise is starting to stop it — and it's starting just where everything in this great country starts — with YOU, the individual consumer. Congratulations. The auto smog control device, the birth control pill, biodegradable toothpaste and now the rectal petcock are all ways that we in business make it our business to help YOU control YOUR pollution.

ECO-MAN. The rectal petcock? Thank you, Capital Growth! And what are you doing about industry?

P. R. MAN. Industry? What about industry?

ECO-MAN. You know — the oil companies — the steel companies — the heavy manufacturing that fills the air and lakes and oceans with smog and crap and goo.

P. R. MAN. Ask yourself a question. What would happen if all the oil drilling stopped, if all the atomic reactors were turned off, if Detroit stopped making gas-burning cars, if there were no more lumbering and freeway building and new cities and new jumbo jet planes?

ECO-MAN. We'd survive. We'd save the world!

P. R. MAN. Uh-uh. America would go down the drain. There'd be no more capital growth. Remember — an economy that isn't expanding can only shrink. And a shrinking economy can only end up — in the red.

World groans.

ECO-MAN. Listen! All this talk! We have to do something!

P. R. MAN. Now you're talking! Let's take a look at the patient. Ah! Why, she doesn't look bad at all. Let's check for fractures. *Feels World.* Hmm. That's a nasty lump. Some kind of artificial cavity there. This part isn't bad — ooh, *excited,* in fact it's outtasight. Whaddya call this country?

ECO-MAN. Alaska. Watch it, will ya? That's virgin territory.

[ECO-MAN]

P. R. MAN. Why sure it is, friend, that's why there's no need to worry — no ecology here — just a lot of — groovy possibilities.

WORLD. *Breathing hard, wakes.* Who? What? EEEK! Eco-Man, get him away, that's the man who took my — who did my — who...*Hysterics.*

P. R. MAN. *Half mounting her.* Easy, baby, easy. Sure, but it's also the man who's gonna fix it all up again.

World screams and faints.

ECO-MAN. Hey, no, listen please, please, let's go back to talking it over.

P. R. MAN. *Smoothing self.* What's that? Why sure! I'll tell ya what we're gonna do. We're gonna have the biggest goddamned ecology fair this beat-up world has ever seen! They'll be picking up candy wrappers and shit for a month! See how it is? When Americans put their heads together, every problem looks a little smaller. *Exits.*

ECO-MAN. O plight of plights! Everything is completely undone! It's the end of the world! Farewell lungs and flowers, eyes and oceans, mountains and taste buds. If there were only some genius, some impartial agency, some school of specialists — wait — school! That's it, that's where the experts are. O Academia, I, Eco-Man, an alumnus, appeal to your biology departments. Send me a specialist before it's too late.

Population Expert enters.
Lab coat, Nazi helmet, German accent.

EXPERT. Solutions! Answers. Feasible alternatives. Viable propositions. Plausible theses. What is the problem, layman? Science has the answer.

ECO-MAN. O Modern Science, repository of truth and objectivity, what please is your impartial analysis of how to save the world? The government gives her poison and free enterprise wants her body!

EXPERT. Laboratory analysis shows that there is only one

valid solution to worldwide pollution, without which
everyone is impotent.

ECO-MAN. Oh, but there IS an answer? Lay it on me quick.

EXPERT. Population control. Birth ban. The pill. Too many
people, not enough earth. Explains all wars, all ideology
merely rationalization. Drop the pill, tie the cords, curb the
impulses, abstain.

ECO-MAN. You mean, if you and I and the other people
stopped having children, there'd be no more problems?

EXPERT. Not quite accurate. You and I, civilized people, not
the problem. Two kids in every crib — stabilize the status
quo, excellent. More precisely the less fortunate, darker
pigmented races, black, yellow, brown, underdeveloped
countries, multiply like guinea pigs, greedy, troublemakers,
too many of 'em. Gotta have birth control. Gotta stop 'em.

ECO-MAN. But how can THEY be the problem when American
Industry has created all the pollution?

EXPERT. Waste makes wealth! Need more machines, less
mouths to feed. Eliminate the poor, no more poverty.

ECO-MAN. But that's genocide. They have a right to live too.

EXPERT. Subjective! For their own good. Why should they live
to starve? Their mere existence threatens the world balance
of power. Threatens peace. You're a pacifist, aren't you?

ECO-MAN. Sure! But even if you eliminated all of them, the
world would still be dying.

EXPERT. But it would be in responsible hands! Final solution
— IUD. *Takes out IUD — huge auto spring — approaches
World.* Or as we sometimes call it, the silent spring. Easy
insertion. Haven't got the lubricant on me, but as Dr. Ehr-
lich says, if they won't do it for themselves, we may have
to do it for 'em; anyway, just gimme a little access to the
underprivileged areas there, and we'll...

WORLD. No!

EXPERT. Own good!

WORLD. Shove it!

EXPERT. Gimme a chance.

WORLD. *Pulls gun.* Eat leaden death!

EXPERT. Eek! *Hollers off.* Warm up the cyclotron, I'm splitting! *Exits.*

ECO-MAN. World! What are you doing? This is no time for violence! Put that gun away!

WORLD. *Rising.* It's no use, Eco-Man. There's only one thing can save me now.

ECO-MAN. What?

WORLD. The only thing that's ever saved me, Eco-Man. The thing I'd die the minute I stopped doing.

ECO-MAN. You mean...?

WORLD. Yes. *Turns.* Revolution. If it weren't for that I'd never have gotten anywhere.

ECO-MAN. But — in your condition?

WORLD. Revolution is my condition, Eco-Man. If the fascists had their way they'd stand me still and keep the sun shining on America 24 hours a day. But that's not the way I work, Eco-Man. I turn ALL my children to the light.

ECO-MAN. But would that save you from pollution?

WORLD. Don't you get it? Pollution is waste, Eco-Man. The only cure for me is no more waste. Re-cycling! Produce only what people can use and use it over and over again. There's no reason not to, except greed. And greed is like speed, Eco-Man. It doesn't matter to a greed-freak if he destroys the world, or even himself, as long as he can make the next connection and put over the next big deal. Who's gonna stop the greed-freaks, Eco-Man? The government won't, private enterprise won't, the universities won't — because that's who they work for. So who does that leave?

ECO-MAN. Nobody — just the people.

WORLD. That's right — the people have to stop it, by any means necessary.

ECO-MAN. But — does it have to be violent?

WORLD. Eco-Man, do you know what Thomas Jefferson said?

ECO-MAN. All women are created equal?

WORLD. *Hits Eco-Man.* No, no — he said, 'God forbid we should be 20 years without a revolution.' That's what he said.

ECO-MAN. And I thought that was a Vista slogan! Forsooth I think we have something, World. I feel more like a human being already, and you —

WORLD. The more we make revolution, the more we make love.

ECO-MAN. World! It's like in the beginning.

Music — 'Love Makes the World Go 'Round.'
They dance.

BERTOLT BRECHT'S
The Mother

A PLAY WITH MUSIC
BY THE
SAN FRANCISCO
MIME TROUPE

268

269

273

"Bring the war home!"
SDS, 1969

A Patriotic Copper Collection Depot:
THE MOTHER carries on
anti-war propaganda.

"As revolutions have begun, it is natural
that other revolutions should follow."
Thomas Paine, 1791

THE MOTHER carries the red flag.

EIGHT SONGS

You Got to Go Out and Get It and Take Yourself Some
Song of the Person Caught in the Middle
Va Terminar
El Corrido de Copper City
The Big Picture
Song of the Nepenthe Flower
Dragon Lady and Blossom Duet
The Banana Song

You Got to go Out and Get It and Take Yourself Some

I dream of a house on top of a hill with
two hap-py chil-dren my clar-ence and Phil. My
hus-band a—do—ores more than my face, and
I'm still a part of the whole hu-man race. But
This is a dream from a dime nov-el—ette, for
sor-row is all that poor wom-en will get. a
hus-band who's bro-ken and drown-ing in gin, and
heart-ache from watch-ing your bab-ies grow thin.

oh

home, home on the range is jump-ing from the fry-ing pan in-to the fi-re. To all my friends of the gen-tle sex : use your brains to save your necks. There's more to life than an ear-ly grave. But you must try try try try — You got to go out and get it and take your self some. 'Cause Eve was a reb-el and she start-ed it all , when she took that fate-ful bite. And Sar-ah Bern-hardt took a chance on that first op-en-ing night. Well what would have hap-pened if Har-i-et Tub-man got off that free-dom train? And what would have hap-pened if Joan of Arc had thought she was in - sane ?

279

280

Song of the Person Caught in the Middle

Hey don't you think this world's a great place!

Hey don't you think that pay - ing your dues pays off.

Hey look at me: worked hard all my life. Stayed in-side the

law—and now I'm on top! And

now I get to be my-self. To stand up and fight for the

right thing. when some hard working man, is robbed of his bread, you

stick your neck out and yell "Stop thief!" SPOKEN: oh yeah. You can be

brave. But watch out. The rewards of honest work make you fearful.
It's better to look the other way, take care

of your own. D.S. al coda

SPOKEN: oh yeah, you can be generous. But watch out. The rewards of honest

work are pretty damn stingy. On a cold winter's night, if someone asks

to share your coat—forget it. Because the choice is a question: of whether

one or both of you will freeze. SUNG: Lord, what's a per-son to

do now. got some-thing to

lose now. The pow-ers that be de-cide the rules: The

deck is stacked, the peo-ple will lose! And there's noth-ing new under the

sun. We're all un-der that same thumb. And I guess the price of cour-

-age is mo-re than I can af-fo-o-o-

-o-o-ord. FINE

282

Va Terminar

© 1977 Javier Pacheco

(salsa)

Lle-
-gar-on con pro-me-sas pre-ten-dien-do sin-cer-i-dad, se ro-bar-on las ri-que-zas y to-mar-on lib-er-tad. Nos o-fre-cier-on su "pro-gre-so," im-pre-sion-an-do la ju-ven-tud, per-o el cos-to fue de in-gres-os, man-ten-ien-do es-clav-i-tud. No, NO, NO es-a in-fam-ia va ter-mi-nar No, NO, NO es-a in-fam-ia va ter-mi-nar No, NO, NO im-per-ial-is-mo se va aca-bar

FINE

El Corrido de Copper City

©1977 Javier Pacheco

Corrido
(Accordion)

En el in - vier-no de la nov-en-ta y nue - ve

en un pueb - li - to por ay en Col - o - ra - do.

To - da la gen-te ha - cien-do sac-ri - fí - cios

que los min - er - os sal - ier-on del tra - ba - jo.

En las de - man-das pi -

- dier-on o-cho ho - ras, y que le pa-gen i-

gual al Mex-i - can - o pero el pa - tron que

man-da no le im-por-ta, man-da-esquir-o- les y

mu-cho di-pu- ta - do.

Coros: Vi - va la huel-ga! The strike in Cop-per Ci - ty,

que to-do el mun-do es-ta por a-po-yar,

aun-que les man-den un tren de es-quir-o- les

la gen-te es fir-me, los van a re-cha- zar.

FINE

The Big Picture

great men, and their hoc-us poc-us.

we be - lieve that folks like us, far a-

-way, who al-so fight, are de-vils

SPOKEN: why can't people see the big picture?

SUNG: But who can blame; peo-ple? Pow-er-ful

men who man-ip-u-late des-pair,

con - trol the press, the schools,

and our im - ag-in-a - tions. Lit-tle pic-tures

are for sale in-stead of in-for-ma-tion. And if you

don't have much, it's hard to take ex-

And a new age, a just, and a beau-ti-ful age, will be brought a-bout by the whole work-ing class. It's so close, and I be-came im-pa-tient.

FINE

Song of the Nepenthe Flower

Tango

Look on the ru-in and rack of gen - e - ra-tions that have gone be - fore. First the Ja-pa-nese, then the French, oo la la la. And now, they tell me, the A - mer - i - can war. So take the sleep of Ne - pen - the — give in. Dream the dream of Ne-pen-the, and float for-e-ver to the sea. So take a look at the ri-ver, as it floats from Long Pihn to the sea.

D.L. SPOKEN: Can you swim against that strong current? CLYDE SPOKEN: Yes!

D.L. SPOKEN: Never ------. sea. FINE

D.S. al coda

291

Dragon Lady and Blossom Duet

D.L.:
1. He won't be the first. I know his two faced kind.
2. I was born to fight. I fought right from the start.

He won't be the last to die be-fore his time.
Some-one cros-ses me I tear the fool a-part.

Bbm/F BASS   Ebm/Db BASS   Bbm/F BASS   Ebm/Db BASS

when I was young I trust-ed a man. He left me flat, did'nt give a damn.

Bbm/F BASS   Ebm/Db BASS   Bbm/F BASS   Ebm/Db BASS

Since that day I've had my way. Since that day I've made my way — A-

F7/C BASS   Bbm7

-lone! **D.L. & Blossom**
1. There're al-ways those who try to make our lives their own. They'll
2. al-ways fed their needs, the men who prey on us, its

get you if they can They'll tear you to the bone. we've
when we've learned their tricks that things be-gin To change.

Bbm/F BASS   Ebm/Db BASS   Bbm/F BASS   Ebm/Db BASS

When you know the moves they make, then you know the moves to take, to

Bbm/F BASS   /Eb BASS   Ebm/Db BASS   /C BASS   F7/C BASS

beat them at their game. I fight **(D.L.)** a-lone
(Blossom) to-gether

D.L. cuts off music:
"Blossom, for one so young, what do you know?"

Bbm

(Flute)

Fm   Bbm/F BASS   Bbm

Blossom:
1. I know what life can be
2. we shared our days to-gether

Fm   Ebm   Bbm

sim-ple har-mo-ny we were of the land
work-ing in green fields moun-tain tops morn-ing mists

Blossom: 1. Then I saw my vil·lage burn·ing, saw my fam·il·y dy·ing,
2. Forced in·to the ci·ty, How we fight to stay a·live.

when we saw the planes re·turn·ing we all left our homes.
So I'm here to work for you — please sol·dier to sur·vive.

D.L.
@ Blossom There're al·ways those who try to make our lives their own. They'll

get you if they can — D.L.: "I'll cut him down, I'll win!"

Bl.: Kil·ling the General is all ve·ry fine Why not see some·thing big·ger this time?

If you were fight·ing for more than your·self, how much great·er your vic·to·ry would be;

D.L.
&
Blossom : "Together"

FINE

The Banana Song

(samba) F   Bb   C7

Help your-self to one nice ba-na-na, ri-pened in our yel-low sun.

C7   F

Feed your cows on our big fish-es, spawned in our blue green sea. The

F   Bb

same old sun shines down on your place, the same old sea comes up to your shore.

Bb   F   C7   F

How come some folks, they got no-thing—some folks, they got more? So

F   Bb   C7

Help your-self to one nice ba-na-na, mean-time we get thin-ner. The

C7   F

land that was used to grow your des-sert had form-er-ly grown our din-ner. For

F   Bb

you ba-na-na is one small thing, you can buy it in a pinch. But

Bb   F   C7   1. F

some-bod-y gets ripped off, you know, when some-bod-y else gets rich. Yes,

2. F   (straight time) Dm7   D7

rich. Is this what you want, the good life at

Gm   C

our ex-pense? No, we don't think so.   We share the

com·mon ex·per·i·ence. You work hard too, and still bare·ly get by. We must ask why things are this way, who wants them, and why? Who wants things this way? Who wants things this way?

(samba)

Mo·ther Earth, she want no·bod·y hun·gry, she made plen·ty beans, ba·na·nas and fish. But some·bod·y gets ripped off, you know, when some·bod·y else gets rich. Yes, rich.

FINE

CREDITS

A NOTE ON CREDITS: All the plays in this book were collective productions in the sense that their content was developed by the company as a whole. The scripts were written in different ways: by one writer, by two or several, by a writer working with performers, by a writer working with a committee. Suggestions and criticism from informed outsiders were always solicited, and often incorporated. Each piece was more or less heavily revised in the course of rehearsal and performance, so the scripts as they appear here bear the mark of the performers and directors as well as the writers. In the same fashion, technicians and musicians contributed to the designs they executed and the music they played. With this disclaimer, credits are given, although they have not appeared in the company's programs.

FALSE PROMISES / NOS ENGAÑARON

Script by Joan Holden, from discussions by the company; *directed* by Arthur Holden, Dan Chumley and Sharon Lockwood; *choreography* by Sharon Lockwood; *designed and executed* by Peggy Snider, Trina Johnson and Patricia Silver. *Stage manager*, Patricia Silver; *researcher*, Merle Goldstone. *Musical director*, Andrea Snow and Bruce Barthol; *incidental music* by Bruce Barthol, Andrea Snow and David Topham; *songs in English* by Andrea Snow, Bruce Barthol and Deb'bora Gilyard, *songs in Spanish* by Javier Pacheco. *Orchestra:* the cast.

CAST:

HARRY/BARBER: Dan Chumley
CHARLIE SLADE/CUSTOMER/MEXICAN MINER/ROUGH RIDER/LIEUTENANT: Barry Levitan
WASHINGTON JEFFERSON: Lonnie Ford
DEPUTY/VOTER/MEXICAN MINER/ROUGH RIDER/MUSICIAN IN PUERTO RICO/ BACKSLIDING MINER: Bruce Barthol
MCKINLEY/CASEY: Ed Levey
MORGAN/BELLE: Melody James
ROOSEVELT/RUBY/2ND DEPUTY: Sharon Lockwood
TOMÁS/STRIKER IN PUERTO RICO: Esteban Oropeza
MONTANA/NEWSVENDOR/MARITZA: Deb'bora Gilyard
MARIA/TOMÁS' FRIEND/BAR LADY IN PUERTO RICO: Marie Acosta, Ilka Payan
2ND ROUGH RIDER/DAVEY: David Topham, Ingrid Monson
MEXICAN WOMAN/BACKSLIDING HOUSEWIFE: Patricia Silver
MORGAN/CUSTOMER: Arthur Holden

SAN FRAN SCANDALS

Script by Steve Friedman and Joan Holden, from a story by Andrea Snow, Melody James and Sharon Lockwood, with Joe Bellan's jokes; *directed and choreographed* by Sharon Lockwood; *designed and executed* by Trina Johnson, Patricia Silver, Peggy Snider, Peter Snider and Denny Partridge Stevens. *Stage manager:* Merle Goldstone, Lonnie Ford. *Music* by Phil Marsh and Andrea Snow; *lyrics* by Phil Marsh and Joan Holden. *Musicians* (not all at once): Jack Wickert, Ted Sobel, Andrea Snow, Barry Levitan, Ed Levey, Arthur Holden, Jay Hamburger, David Topham, Jim Kaufmann, Jeff Unger.

CAST:
STELLA: Melody James
FRANK: Dan Chumley, Ed Levey
SNEATH/CARLOTTA SNOTTA: Ed Levey, Andrea Snow
FARQUHAR: Joan Mankin, Sharon Lockwood
SMELLYBUCKS: Paul Binder, Arthur Holden
Special note: STELLA was originally JOE, played by Joe Bellan. CARLOTTA
SNOTTA was HOWARD HUGE, played by Andrea Snow.

THE DRAGON LADY'S REVENGE

Script by Joan Holden, Patricia Silver, Andrea Snow and Jael Weisman;
directed by Denny Partridge Stevens and Jael Weisman, with Dan Chumley;
designed and executed by Peggy Snider, Peter Snider, Trina Johnson, Patricia
Silver, Dan Chumley and Denny Partridge Stevens. *Stage manager:* Peter Snider,
Trina Johnson, Denny Partridge Stevens, Patricia Silver, Joan Holden, Merle
Goldstone. *Music* by Randall Craig, Barry Glick, Andrea Snow, Theodore

Sobel, Jack Wickert; *lyrics* by Randall Craig, Barry Glick, Jael Weisman. *Musicians:* Jack Dowding, Harvey Robb, Theodore Sobel, Jack Wickert, Larry Pisoni, Ed Levey, Michael Christensen.

CAST:
HAROLD: Larry Pisoni, Jack Dowding
CLYDE: Michael Christensen, Ed Levey
DROOLEY: Jael Weisman, Michael Christensen
TRAN DOG: Randall Craig, Dan Chumley, Paul Binder, Bennett Yahya
AMBASSADOR: Jason Harris, Arthur Holden
RONG Q: Joan Mankin, Sharon Lockwood
BLOSSOM: Sharon Lockwood, Melody James
DRAGON LADY: Andrea Snow

THE INDEPENDENT FEMALE

Script by Joan Holden, with grateful acknowledgement to the San Francisco Bay Area women's movement; *directed* by Sandra Archer and Denny Partridge Stevens; *designed and executed* by Peggy Snider, Peter Snider, Patricia Silver and Denny Partridge Stevens. *Stage manager:* Peter Snider, Patricia Silver, Denny Partridge Stevens, Joan Holden. *Music* by Jack Wickert. *Musicians:* Jack Wickert, Jack Dowding, Theodore Sobel, Harvey Robb.

CAST:
THE BARKER: Dan Chumley, Michael Christensen
MOM: Joe Bellan, Jason Harris, Andrea Snow
GLORIA: Joan Mankin
JOHN: Randall Craig
SARAH: Sharon Lockwood
WALTER: Lorne Berkun, Steve Friedman, Jack Dowding

FRIJOLES

Script by Joan Holden, Sharon Lockwood, Patricia Silver and Andrea Snow; *directed* by Sharon Lockwood; *designed and executed* by Trina Johnson and Patricia Silver. *Stage manager:* David Topham. *Music* by Andrea Snow and David Topham; *lyrics* by Andrea Snow. *Musicians:* Bruce Barthol, Barry Levitan, Jeff Unger and the cast.

CAST:
PEPE: Lonnie Ford, Ed Robledo
CONCHITA: Marie Acosta
PATRÓN/WAITER: Esteban Oropeza, Sharon Lockwood

[CREDITS]

BUNZ: Arthur Holden
KISSINGER/HAMBURGER EATERS: Ed Levey, Sharon Lockwood
PHYLLIS: Andrea Snow, Sharon Lockwood
HARRY: Dan Chumley
WESTERN UNION MAN: David Topham, Bruce Barthol, Ingrid Monson

FROZEN WAGES

Script by the cast, Richard Benetar, Dan Chumley and Joan Holden; *directed* by Dan Chumley; *designed and executed* by Larry Pisoni, Peggy Snider, Trina Johnson and Denny Partridge Stevens. *Music:* anonymous; *musicians:* the cast and Jack Wickert.

CAST:
MYRTLE: Merle Goldstone
GONZALES: Michael Nolan
NORMAN: Michael Christensen
RICHARD: Larry Pisoni
BETTY: Peggy Snider, Melody James
ROSIE: Joan Mankin, Sharon Lockwood
MR. BEAVER: John Condrin, Jason Harris
NEP ANGEL: Jack Dowding, Andrea Snow, Patricia Silver

LOS SIETE

Script by Steve Friedman; *directed* by Jael Weisman; *drawings* by Dan Chumley and Rebecca Schiffren; *engineering* by Peter Snider.

CAST:
BART: Steve Friedman, Dan Chumley, Jason Harris, Andrea Snow
PASSENGER: Dan Chumley, Jack Dowding, Theodore Sobel, Jael Weisman

ECO-MAN

Script by Steve Friedman; *directed* by Jael Weisman; *designed and executed* by Peggy Snider and Peter Snider. *Musicians:* Theodore Sobel, Jack Wickert.

CAST:
THE WORLD: Sandra Archer, Melody James, Sharon Lockwood, Joan Mankin, Andrea Snow
ECO-MAN: Dan Chumley
GOVERNMENT/PR/POPULATION CONTROL: Steve Friedman, Jael Weisman, Joe

Bellan, Jason Harris, Arthur Holden, Bennett Yahya
Special note: ECO-MAN later became ECO-GIRL, played by Sharon Lockwood, Joan Mankin

THE MOTHER, by Bertolt Brecht

Directed by Dan Chumley and Denny Partridge Stevens; *designed and executed* by Peggy Snider, Trina Johnson and Patricia Silver. *Stage manager:* Patricia Silver, Trina Johnson, Merle Goldstone, Steve Friedman, Peter Snider, Denny Partridge Stevens. *Musical Director:* Andrea Snow; *music* by Hans Eisler, Barry Glick, Phil Marsh, Andrea Snow, Theodore Sobel and Jack Wickert. *Musicians:* Barry Levitan, Theodore Sobel, Jack Wickert, Ed Levey, Arthur Holden, Andrea Snow, David Topham, Jim Kaufmann, Jeff Unger.

The following performers appeared in the following roles:
Dan Chumley: IVAN/SOSTAKOVITCH/THE BUTCHER/SECOND WORKER/WOMAN WORKER
Lonnie Ford: IVAN/SOSTAKOVITCH/YEGOR LUSHIN/KITCHEN HELPER/FIRST WORKER
Jay Hamburger: PAVEL/STRIKEBREAKER/WOMAN WORKER/BOURGEOIS WOMAN
Arthur Holden: THE COMMISSIONER/GATEKEEPER/THE TEACHER/YEGOR LUSHIN/KITCHEN HELPER/FIRST WORKER/WOUNDED SOLDIER
Melody James: KATYA (MASHA)/BUTCHER'S WIFE/LANDLADY/WOMAN WITH CHILD/BOURGEOIS WOMAN/YOUNG MAID
Ed Levey: KARPOV/SMILGIN/POLICEMAN/PRISON GUARD/STRIKEBREAKER/PAVEL'S COMRADE/CHILD/BOURGEOIS WOMAN
Barry Levitan: COMPANY POLICEMAN/STRIKEBREAKER
Sharon Lockwood: THE MOTHER
Joan Mankin: CHORUS LEADER/A WORKER/MRS. SOSTAKOVITCH/KITCHEN HELPER/SHOPKEEPER/TENANT/WOMAN IN BLACK
Esteban Oropeza: PAVEL/KITCHEN HELPER/BOURGEOIS WOMAN
Andrea Snow: POLICEMAN/THE BUTCHER/SHOPKEEPER/BOURGEOIS WOMAN
Theodore Sobel: WORKER/COMPANY POLICEMAN
Jeff Unger: POLICEMAN/WORKER

These shows were booked by Jael Weisman, Denny Partridge Stevens, Michael Nolan, Paul Binder, Joan Mankin, Sharon Lockwood, Melody James, Arthur Holden, Lonnie Ford and Jay Moss; publicity by Linda Post, Merle Goldstone, Andrea Snow, Esteban Oropeza and Angus Mackenzie.

The San Francisco Mime Troupe was founded in 1959 by R. G. Davis, who was director of the company until 1970.

FOR THE BOOK

Editor: Peter Solomon
Designer: Charles A. Bigelow
Production Manager: Kris Holmes
Typesetters: Martin White and Patti Morris, Irish Setter
Printer: Mastercraft Press, Inc.

Cover Design: Rene Yung
Cover Photo: Ron Blanchette

FALSE PROMISES/NOS ENGAÑARON
  Poster: Jane Norling
  Photographs:
    Pages 15, 39, 47, 53, 64, 77: Marian Beth Goldman
    Page 18: Mike Fellner
    Pages 19, 21, 28, 34, 48, 49, 57, 68, 79: Ron Blanchette
    Pages 23, 25, 26, 50: Tom Copi
    Page 58: Gerhard Gscheidle
    Page 75: Ted Shank
    Page 81: a friend in France*
SAN FRAN SCANDALS
  Poster: Susan Lyne
  Photographs: Mara Sabinson
THE DRAGON LADY'S REVENGE
  Poster: Patrick Lofthouse
  Photographs:
    All by Howie Epstein, except
    Page 121: Bob Hobby*
    Page 125: Gerhard Gscheidle
THE INDEPENDENT FEMALE
  Poster: photograph by Jonathan Ezekiel
  Photographs: Gerhard Gscheidle
STAGES OF THE STAGE
  Photographs: Marian Beth Goldman
  Drawings: Trina Johnson
FRIJOLES
  Photographs:
    Pages 207, 217: Yasha Aginsky
    Page 211: Valerie Vogel
    Page 216: Ron Blanchette
    Page 220: Marian Beth Goldman
    Page 229: Daniel Hunter
FROZEN WAGES
  Photographs:
    Pages 234, 242: Anonymous*
    Page 235: Roger Lubin
LOS SIETE
  Drawings: Rebecca Schiffren and
    Dan Chumley
ECO-MAN
  Photographs: Anonymous*
THE MOTHER
  Poster: Jane Norling
  Photographs: Tom Copi
MUSIC
  Photograph: Mara Sabinson
  Scores: penned by David Topham
CREDITS
  Photographs:
    Page 296: Angus MacKenzie
    Page 298: Mara Sabinson

*Despite every effort we could not discover the names or addresses of some
photographers. Any assistance along these lines greatly appreciated.